UNSETTLING THE WORD

Biblical Experiments in Decolonization

Edited by
Steve Heinrichs

ORBIS BOOKS
Maryknoll, New York 10545

Fourth Printing, November 2021

ORBIS BOOKS
Maryknoll, New York 10545

Fathers and Brothers
MARYKNOLL™

Unsettling the Word: Biblical Experiments in Decolonization
Copyright © 2018 Mennonite Church Canada
First U.S. edition published in 2019 by Orbis Books

Editor: Steve Heinrichs
Copy Editor: Kyla Neufeld
Design & Layout: Jonathan Dyck
Publisher: Mennonite Church Canada

Royalties from *Unsettling the Word* will be sent to Christian Peacemaker Teams to support the work of Indigenous Peoples Solidarity (IPS). Enlisting faith groups, Settlers and other non-Indigenous groups, IPS builds partnerships with Indigenous nations, communities and movements engaged in decolonization, seeking justice, and defending the land against corporate and government exploitation. For more information, see cpt.org

Library of Congress Cataloging-in-Publication Data

Names: Heinrichs, Steve (Director of Indigenous-Settler Relations), editor.
Title: Unsettling the word : biblical experiments in decolonization / edited
   by Steve Heinrichs.
Description: First U.S. edition. | Maryknoll : Orbis Books, 2018. | Includes
   bibliographical references and index.
Identifiers: LCCN 2018041128 | ISBN 9781626983113 (pbk.)
Subjects: LCSH: Bible--Postcolonial criticism. | Postcolonialism. |
   Decolonization.
Classification: LCC BS521.86 .U57 2018 | DDC 220.6--dc23 LC record available at
https://lccn.loc.gov/2018041128

FOR GENERATIONS, the Bible has been employed by settler colonial societies as a weapon to dispossess Indigenous and racialized peoples of their lands, cultures, and spiritualities. Given this devastating legacy, many want nothing to do with it. But is it possible for the exploited and their allies to reclaim the Bible from the dominant powers? Can we make it an instrument for justice in the cause of the oppressed? Even a nonviolent weapon toward decolonization?

In *Unsettling the Word,* over 60 Indigenous and Settler authors come together to wrestle with the Scriptures, re-reading and re-imagining the ancient text for the sake of reparative futures.

Created by Mennonite Church Canada's Indigenous-Settler Relations program, *Unsettling the Word* is intended to nurture courageous conversations with the Bible, our current settler colonial contexts, and the Church's call to costly peacemaking. To order additional copies, please visit: orbisbooks.com

CONTENTS

Contents

LIBERATING THE BIBLE

Steve Heinrichs

Instead of giving the Bible back to the colonizers, why don't we "make it our own"?

— Pablo Richard, Chilean theologian

IT'S SHORTLY AFTER DAWN, and I'm sitting in a barley field, cold hands clumsily thumbing through the pages of my pocket Bible. Scarf wrapped tight, hot tea by my side, I've come to this quiet place to read and to pray. But I'm struggling. Today's text is a wild story about David, a brash young Israelite king who believes the Philistines are occupying his promised land (2 Samuel 5). David asks God if he should take up arms against these peoples. And God's response? "Go for it!"

Disturbed by this ancient word, tempted to skip it in favour of a praise psalm or a Jesus-teaching, I ask for help. "Lord, speak to me. What am I to do with this?"

Suddenly, I see two camouflage Humvees driving down the nearby "Settler Only" highway. My gut tells me they're going to stop. And they do. Screeching to an abrupt halt, doors fling open, and a half-dozen armed soldiers from the Israeli Defense Forces get out and start marching towards me through the field — a generations-old Palestinian field. My heart begins to race. For a second, I consider texting my Christian Peacemaker Team colleagues so I won't have to face this situation alone. But I don't. I just clutch my Bible and sit tight. Within a minute, I'm surrounded on all sides, and the captain of this brigade asks — in curt yet smooth English — "What are you doing here?"

Nervous, I look him in the eyes and gently respond, "Reading my Bible."

The soldiers exchange glances. Most laugh. It's not the answer they were anticipating.

"But why are you here? You're a foreigner!" the captain says dismissively. "You don't belong in this place!"

Gripping my Bible even tighter, I launch into my story. "I've come to the village of At-Tuwani because the Jewish Settlers of Ma'on, the Israeli government, and you soldiers, are taking their land. I've come from Canada to stand against this injustice, to stand up for peace, and to stand in solidarity with my Muslim sisters and brothers."

I hear my voice and realize I'm rather animated. But I keep on.

"I've travelled thousands of miles to be here, because I believe the God of the Bible is a God of nonviolence and liberation," I declare, holding up my blue-black leather book. "A God who defends the oppressed against the powerful! A God who desires the well-being of all peoples! A God who will not tolerate the greed of nations who devour the poor for their gain! That's why I'm here!"

The soldiers fidget and exchange another set of looks. Some raise their eyebrows. Others smirk. Then one opines, with the approval of the group, "If you knew your Bible, you'd know that this is our land. God gave it to us."

I could have laughed. "*If you knew your Bible...*" It's as if they knew what I had been reading and wrestling with this morning and were calling me on it. But I don't feel like laughing. I feel heavy. I want to curse and cry. How did these men and women, not much younger than I, get to this damnable place where they believe God is a champion of settler colonialism? A divine warrior who blesses favourites by stealing the lands and lives of others?

Speechless, I sit before the soldiers, staring at the Bible in my hands. I love this book. It has gifted me in so many ways, offering "a lamp to my feet, and a light to my path" (Psalm 119:105). But I know that it's also a dangerous book, one that can fuel great harm and violence, even genocide. And right now, in this moment, I would like to bring this Bible of mine low to the ground, place it before the feet of these machine-gun toting soldiers, and, with tears of grief, tear out all those damaging texts that breathe oppressive imagination and action. Then—and only then—I'll lift it high, imploring their eyes, mine too, to behold the better parts. Those of beauty, compassion, and costly solidarity. Those which offer a better God who speaks, "Love your neighbour as yourself," "Blessed are the peacemakers," "Do justice, love mercy, and walk humbly." A God who empties God's very self to suffer with the suffering. A God who "will wipe every tear from their eyes"—Israelite and Philistine eyes, Jewish and Palestinian eyes, Settler and Indigenous eyes.

But I make no move. I just sit there, in silence, shaking before my Bible.

The soldiers stare at me with curiosity. A minute or so later, a few Hebrew imperatives are uttered, and they're gone.

¤

It's been 10 years since that disquieting encounter took place in the South Hebron Hills of the West Bank, and the questions I had around the Bible then are the questions I continue to grapple with today: How do we read this book so that it is a force for justice and peace in the cause of the oppressed? How do we—particularly those who come to the sacred page with a posture of trust, a hermeneutic of love—become more attentive to and honest about the contested traditions, competing theologies, and clash of ideologies that are present in this canon of writings? And if we, who claim the Bible as part of our communal identity, affirm our ethical responsibility to live into the best of Scripture's streams of justice… what then is our responsibility when it comes to those toxic streams of violence that have been employed over the centuries as weapons of mass destruction, streams that are still used today? *Unsettling the Word: Biblical Experiments in Decolonization* is an effort to explore and engage these kinds of questions.

The inspiration for this work came to me last summer. As my kids played in a Winnipeg waterpark, I sat in the grass reading James Cone's magnificent *The Cross and the Lynching Tree*. Cone, a black liberation theologian, argues that the white church in America needs to experience a radical conversion so that they might see more clearly, or maybe for the first time, who God is… see what blacks have seen and sung about for generations: that the God of the crucified Jesus is found in the suffering of black women and men. Cone's not saying that God is simply present amidst the suffering of the oppressed—something most, if not all, Christians would affirm. It's a more far-reaching assertion. God actually identifies the suffering of blacks as God's very own. So who is God in the United States? Who is God in a country where thousands of black bodies have been strung up on trees as a result of white supremacy and domination? God is the lynched black body. Cone writes:

> God saw what whites did to innocent and helpless blacks and claimed their suffering as God's own. God transformed lynched black bodies into the recrucified body of Christ. *Every time a white mob lynched a black person, they lynched Jesus....*
>
> The lynching tree is a metaphor for white America's crucifixion of black people. It is the window that best reveals the religious meaning of the cross in our land. In this sense, black people are Christ figures, not because they wanted to suffer but because they had no choice. Just as Jesus had no choice in his journey to Calvary, so black people had no choice about being lynched. The evil forces of the Roman state and of white supremacy in America willed it. Yet, God took the evil of the cross and the lynching tree and transformed them both into the triumphant beauty of the divine.

Cone's claim might strike some ears as extreme. Yet what he's doing—seeing God in the oppressed—is nothing new. It's rooted in startling biblical traditions like Isaiah 53's Suffering Servant, where God is encountered in the bruised victim rejected by the people. It's rooted in subversive texts like Matthew 25's "whatever you do unto the least—the poor, the hungry, the imprisoned—you do unto me [the Christ]." And it's built on the witness, experience, and imagination of generations of resilient black poets, preachers, and prophets. People like W. E. B. Du Bois (c. 1868–1963) who, in the words of Cone, pointed to a "Black Christ in a land lighted by the burning crosses of the Ku Klux Klan." In fact, it was the witness of Du Bois that really got me thinking about the particular shape of this project.

Back in the 1910s and '20s, Du Bois—a sociologist and activist who co-founded the National Association for the Advancement of Coloured People—was distressed by the deafening silence of the white church in response to overwhelming black pain and injustice. "Who is the God that such a church sees and worships?" Du Bois asks. "How do these white Christians read their Bible? And how can that be transformed?"

One of the strategies that Du Bois takes up to speak into this scandalous context is a redeployed Bible. But it's no ordinary Bible; it's been radicalized. Du Bois takes the ancient words treasured by white and black Christian alike and re-visions them into the contemporary environs—the word made fresh to build up a battered black church; the word made fresh to tear down walls of hellish segregation in the white church. And so we read of a young white Mary who gives birth to a black baby Christ in the land of Georgia; a black Christ who grows up to preach in and amongst the plantation poor a message of fundamental equality and justice; a black Christ who is executed by the State of Mississippi at the instigation of a dominant church who accuse him of blaspheming "the White Race"; a black Christ who's sign of salvation is the noosed rope.

These were deeply challenging stories that Du Bois lifted up before the eyes and ears of the watching world. To appreciate just how explosive his accounts were, consider by comparison the Jesus offered up by Clarence Jordan (c. 1912–1969)—the white Christian who founded Koinonia, an interracial farming community in Georgia. Jordon created his own re-visioned Bible, the *Cotton Patch Gospel*, in which his Jesus, like Du Bois', goes around preaching a revolutionary inclusive message in the Southern States. Jordan's Jesus, like Du Bois', is also put to death by the white state in cahoots with the white church. And Jordan's Jesus, like Du Bois', is crucified on the lynching tree. But Jordan's Jesus, unlike Du Bois', is white.

Perhaps Jordan believed that Jesus needed to be white in order to be consistent in his re-visioning of the New Testament story. If the Temple and Pharisees are the white Christian establishment, then Jesus should be white too. Or perhaps this white Jesus was a concession that Jordan made in order to reach his intended audience. Maybe he believed it would be too hard for the white Christian to see, to fully identify "God in the flesh" with a black human being. But not Du Bois, for that's exactly where God is to be found. Christ is in the lynched black body. And our healing and salvation—the collective well-being of black and white and all peoples—is dependent upon our seeing it. God is the God of the oppressed.

Reading Cone and Du Bois got me thinking about my Canadian context. What would the word made fresh look like here? Over the last decade, churches in this northern portion of Turtle Island have been called to action by Indigenous peoples like never before. Called through the Truth and Reconciliation Commission on Indian Residential Schools. Called through grassroots movements like Idle No More. Called to stand up for justice with Indigenous nations. Called to stand against destructive forces of state exploitation and corporate extraction.

Yet we Christians have also been called to take a good hard look at ourselves. To reflect on our Christian beliefs, to scrutinize our missional practices. And to decolonize. It's not that Christianity is inherently colonial, but for generations the Church and its faith have been used—wittingly, unwittingly, and far too often—as instruments of dispossession in the settler colonial arsenal. Indigenous peoples are asking the Church to do our own work, to beat our colonial swords into peaceable ploughshares.

As I sat in the lush grass by that Winnipeg water park, on land treatied *and* taken from the Cree, Anishinaabe, and Dakota; as I watched my kids play in the life-giving water stolen from the people of Shoal Lake 40 First Nation; I contemplated Du Bois' biblical strategy of speaking truth to power. What if we tried to do something similar here? What if we sought to unsettle the sacred stories of the Church for today? Could this be a way to do our decolonization homework? Could this help us see and follow the crucified peoples of this land? Holding Cone's book tight, thumbing pages warmed in the hot sun, I quietly said a prayer. "Creator, speak to me. What should we do?"

Over the next months, I sent a pitch to a wide range of Indigenous and Settler authors, poets, and grassroots activists. I asked if they'd like to join me in "courageously making the old biblical word flesh in today's settler colonial context(s)... offering gritty and experimental reflections that can be used in pulpit and street to surprise, stir, and startle us into seeing the prophetic word anew and strange." More than 60 responded, an amazing circle of contributors from rich and diverse spiritual backgrounds—Christian, Jewish, traditional Indigenous, and animist. They come from across Canada and the U.S., from Africa, Australia, and the U.K., and together, they offer up a powerful set of riffs on classic Scripture texts.

Some, like Du Bois, boldly re-imagine the old stories to offer a word of freedom for today's sinned-against. Others take a different tack and seek to expose the violence of specific texts, laying them bare so that all might see, confess, and embrace a better way. A number offer radical commentary with pointed calls to action. And a few can do nothing—or everything!—but pray the text back to us, to the land, and to God.

The Bible has been used as a tool of colonialism, xenophobia, exclusion, and cultural genocide. It still is. But this does not have to be. For centuries, communities of radical compassion and courage have read and re-read the sacred page in creative and critical fashion, so that these old memories shake the powers from their thrones and bring actual change to those who have been kept down. My prayer is that *Unsettling the Word* will be a helpful and encouraging resource to those who are running in that holy tradition—and those who want to join it. My prayer is that this book will inspire people to take up the Scriptures, read them again, and conduct their own experiments in speaking fresh words into their worlds. And my prayer, above all, is that our hearts will be so stirred, our minds so lovingly unsettled by what we encounter in this text, that we are moved to works of mercy, risks of solidarity, and costly acts of reparative love. The Bible must be lived (and enjoyed) in streams of justice, or it is a dead word.

In the 1960s, Jomo Kenyatta (c. 1897–1978), an anti-colonial activist who became Prime Minister and President of Kenya, popularised the following aphorism about the Bible, a pithy shock-summary of Christian imperialism that's been appropriated by many Indigenous peoples around the world.

When the missionaries arrived, the Africans had the land and the missionaries had the Bible. They taught us how to pray with our eyes closed. When we opened them, they had the land and we had the Bible.

I've heard this saying, made specific to the Canadian situation, a dozen or more times at different reconciliation gatherings. It contains important truths—hard truths. And when people hear it, they often laugh, not too loud, but in a "that's-funny-and-so-sad" kind of way. But I dream of

a day when we can recast that word. I dream of a day when thousands
upon thousands of churches, and all those who claim the Biblical tradition, will link arms with grassroots and frontline communities to reverse
the trajectory of that saying!

This is the dream that I hear in black theologian Itumeleng Mosala
and so many others: "The task now…is to enable [the oppressed] to use
the Bible to get the land back and to get the land back without losing
the Bible." For that to happen, for the oppressed to experience a Jubilee
of reparation, the Bible itself—Mosala underscores—will need to be
liberated. It is through a critical appropriation of the sacred texts and its
stories, a fearless re-reading of the Bible through the eyes of the exploited, that this old book can be made a holy, nonviolent weapon in today's
struggle to "get the land back."

May it be.

Come Holy Spirit,
speak your word anew.
Move among us!
And move us.

God saw everything that he had made, and indeed, it was very good. And there was evening and there was morning, the sixth day.

Genesis 1:31

RETURN TO THE GOOD

Marcus Briggs-Cloud

SHOULD YOU WALK into a Maskoke church service of any denomination, you're guaranteed to hear exhortations evoking heavenly "streets of gold" and "many mansions." These are goals, we are told, to which we should aspire in our spiritual journey. We must, of course, restrain ourselves from confronting the fact that this otherworldly gold is mined from the sacred lands of the Shoshone People. Or that tens of thousands of gold-panning Indigenous African child labourers harvest the finite commodity. And forget the fact that each mine supplying those gold streets depends on millions of gallons of sacred water—pumped each and every day—that won't percolate back into an aquifer fast enough to avoid violent wars over limited access to our first medicine. We'll also ignore that those many mansion frames are built with lumber unsustainably harvested from the Amazon forest, an ecosystem from which Indigenous Peoples and countless species are currently being displaced due to habitat loss through deforestation.

How did a realm of capitalism, dependent on an extractive economy that exists at the expense of the natural world, become the most desired place for one to exist? What happened to all that genuine "good" stuff we learned about way back at our genesis—the beginning of our human consciousness—back before our spirits were fogged by material culture?

Recall the images: plants yielding seed, fruits of every kind; birds flying in the air, soaring over the many land-crawling and sea-dwelling beings. One would think that God said it was "good" enough times that we wouldn't have forgotten what is "good" enough.

In my Maskoke language, the most esteemed compliments and

3

affirmations are various derivatives of the word *heretv*, a simultaneous infinitive verb and noun "to be good/goodness." Nothing feels better than to hear an elder remark on one's action with the conjugated form *heremahetos* (very good). The profound depth of *heretv* in Maskoke cannot be approximated in English without a deeper Maskoke cultural competency, but simply put, any good Maskoke person actively strives to meet the mark of all that *heretv* conceptually encompasses. But we're forgetting that too.

Some years ago, I was gathered with teenage peers in the presence of an elder sharing traditional teachings, when he paused mid-story to ask us the name of the tree we were sitting under. After a few seconds of embarrassing silence, we were chastised for having been around this living being for an extended period and not knowing its name. Our lack of consciousness of whose roots we were sitting upon was nothing short of shameful, and needless to say, did not merit an encouraging *heremahe*. Among us Maskoke People, this is all-too-common. We have forgotten what is "good."

Our Indigenous language, the gateway to understanding the world around us as Maskoke People, has evolved in a co-evolutionary manner within localized ecosystems into which our ancestors were integrated. So it is through our Indigenous language that we are inherently tied to our genesis—that which is "good." It will take some effort, but walk slowly with me to see these intricacies.

The evolution of our Indigenous language can be illustrated through a study of etymological relationships between the Maskoke words *vhakv*, interpreted as "law," and *vhake*, referring to a copy or imitation of something. These two words descend from the same source: that is, the natural order. Possessing only one different letter (the final letter), both terms are ecological in origin.

Maskoke *vhakv* (law) comes from the replication of phenomena in the natural order within the contiguous Maskoke bioregion. The word *hake* conjures an active verb mode of mirroring another entity, whereas uttering its nominalized form *hakv* converts the meaning to elucidate a collective perception of the biogeographical ecosystem. Still with me? The first letter, "v," serves as a locative prefix marker, placing the noun vertically in attachment to another entity. So, in this case, abidance of *vhakv* (law) means to attach Maskoke People to

4

the natural order through observance and imitation of local non-human ecology.

Maskoke People then implement cultural regulations based on observed natural order. As you all know, ecosystems regulate themselves extraordinarily, even down to micronutrient inputs and outputs. Hence, when they're not subject to anthropogenic harm, ecosystems maintain balance. And that is the goal of Maskoke society. *Vhakv* (law) — the agent that enforces egalitarian ideology within Maskoke society — is patterned after Maskoke Peoples' understanding of balance and equity within the natural order.

Unlike me and my peers, who weren't able to name the tree that was gifting us with shade, oxygen, and presence, it's clear that my ancestors have always been keen observers of that which is "good." Our language and culture, so deeply shaped by an ecological worldview, witnesses such. And yet, this rich and beautiful language is projected to fall silent in 25 years.

Having established that Maskoke governance emerged from an imitation of ecological balance, we should also acknowledge prescribed gender roles deriving from that same balance. We find this in the story of the Corn Woman, a woman who is the sole progenitor of maize. Corn is the most sacred food in Maskoke society, a gift for which profound sacrificial thanks is given during annual ceremonies called *Posketv* (Green Corn Dance) that renew our relationships to the natural world. Since this sacred food was left to the People by a woman, the descendant Maskoke caretakers of this crop are women. This responsibility bestows great importance on the value of women as stewards of something profoundly sacred.

Regrettably, settler colonialism deeply severed this sacred connection, as government appointed Indian agents removed women from the fields and put them in homes to fulfill domesticated roles modelled by European women. This hegemonic patriarchal campaign stripped women of their vital role, not only in maintaining survival through cultivation of food sustenance, but also in cultivating the source of Maskoke spirituality.

Today, 39 percent of our women experience domestic violence. Today, we don't even grow corn as a part of our "Green Corn Dance" ceremonies. Instead of maintaining an egalitarian complex reinforced by our own agricultural practices and ceremonies, we allow multinational corporations to care for the seeds and fruits of the earth; they control our food systems and further widen the socio-economic equity gap. We witness rapid genetic engineering of those "good" seeds and "good" fruits in laboratories after our Indigenous ancestors spent thousands of years spiritually caring for them through sacrificial and thanksgiving rituals. Today, my people have forgotten how to do agriculture. That is not good.

Decolonization requires returning to what is "good." I coordinate an intentional Indigenous Maskoke ecovillage community *Ekvn-Yefolecv* (ee-gun yee-full-lee-juh) that practices cultural, linguistic, and ecological sustainability. Embodying a double entendre in the Maskoke language — returning to the earth and returning to our homelands — *Ekvn-Yefolecv* reclaimed a piece of our ancestral homeland in Alabama from which we were forcibly removed in 1836 and relocated 700 miles away. We work to protect sacred seeds and sacred fruits and to re-empower women through organic farming, we practice conservation of endangered fish and other animal species, and we revitalize Maskoke language through immersion methodologies among our children.

We are remembering that our songs came from birds and land crawlers; remembering to sing them now with deeper cognizance of ecological sustainability and concern for what it would be like to not have them on this earth. We are relearning names and ways of the birds, fish, bugs, plants, and other biota in the ecosystems with whom we share.

It was in the beginning that we were taught what is "good." We're finding our way back there, to the natural world, and so finding ourselves again. It is time that we all reclaim our genesis. We must intimately interact with what is "good" in order to effectively enact what is good.

The LORD saw that the wickedness of humankind was great in the earth, and that every inclination of the thoughts of their hearts was only evil continually. And the LORD was sorry that he had made humankind on the earth, and it grieved him to his heart.

Genesis 6:5–6

GOODNESS TURNS

Christina Conroy

I can feel the water.
It rises to my lowest branches.

My skin opens to the rain and I flood the air with fragrance. A gift of beauty; my refusal to participate in the diminishing of goodness.

There is no goodness left, says the Lord. It was a mistake to make humans, says the Lord. We must start again, says the Lord.

I do not need the humans to survive. I and the rest of creation will flourish without them. Yet I have been watching. I have attended to their comings and goings for hundreds of years. I look among them. I look on the weak. I look on the strong. I see and love. I extend my branches to the sky, higher than all other trees, that I may honour their wounds. They are fragile, these humans. They are small and they do not have good sight. They do not see that their Creator is ever near. They do not see me.

The Lord senses my protest. Punishment is the language of humans, I tell the Lord. By this they will understand their wickedness, but not that their wickedness betrays the Good who created them, the Goodness whose image they bear. You are angry, I tell the Lord. If you spare only some, you will teach them to destroy. They will think anger on earth is eternally upheld. They will take it upon themselves to condemn others. And they will enact that condemnation with great violence, serving might instead of mercy.

Goodness is silent.
Goodness turns.
I can feel the water.
It rises to my highest branches.
I am tall and old. I will stay with those whom I have seen.
The flora holds me. I hold the others,
the insects and the birds, all creatures that swarm the earth.
We receive the rain together.

I hear a great sound like I have never heard before, the sound of a great split into the heart of Love itself. God sees the choking earth and weeps for the suffering of creation. God sees Noah.

And Goodness turns again.

God's rains sink deep into the earth. I extend one branch to the sky for the dove to find rest. I extend one branch for the Lord to see.

We must start again, says the Lord. My promise was not enough, says the Lord. They will be wicked again, but harm will not answer harm. I will never curse ground nor destroy every living creature again. You are tall and old, and you will show them. You will look on the weak among them. You will look on the strong. You will see and love.

> I am establishing my covenant with you and your descendants after you, and with every living creature that is with you, the birds, the domestic animals, and every animal of the earth with you, as many as came out of the ark. I establish my covenant with you, that never again shall all flesh be cut off by the waters of a flood, and never again shall there be a flood to destroy the earth (Genesis 9: 8–11).

Above us and around us — the survivors, the community of creation — appear the colours that make the light, the fragrances that delight the heart, the rhythms that heal the earth. The colours arc around us, enfolding us, holding us all together. This is the sign that Goodness turns from destruction, says the Lord. This is the sign that teaches you to say, "never again." This is the sign of the covenant

between Goodness and every living creature for all future generations,
says the Lord.

I can feel the water.
My roots run deep and strong.
I do not need the humans to survive.
But they too are created good.
They come to me for air and shade.
I extend my branches to the sky,
higher than all other trees,
that I may honour their wounds.

And they said to one another, "Come, let us make bricks, and burn them thoroughly." And they had brick for stone, and bitumen for mortar. Then they said, "Come, let us build ourselves a city, and a tower with its top in the heavens, and let us make a name for ourselves."

Genesis 11:3—4

THE FOOLISHNESS OF PETROPOLIS

Steve Heinrichs

OUR STORY COMES from the Middle East, great Babylon, and it comes from here, colonial Canada, the Petropolis state. The story goes back to the near beginnings, to the Genesis gone amok. And it goes something like this.

At one time, all the people of the world spoke the same language and used the same words.

Check that. Not all the people, but principally the wealthy people and the white people. Those folks and the many they co-opted spoke the same imperial language and employed the same deadly logic. Powerful words like *capital, progress, property, stocks* and *bonds*; powerful ideas like *free markets, human resources, natural resources, bang for the buck, secure energy, collateral damage, freedom of choice, freedom 55; all you can eat, all you can wear, all you can watch, all you can fuck*—anytime, all the time, anywhere.

Now these people were often on the move, looking to the east, to the south, and to the west, trying to secure their well-being by securing more lands, more waters, more jobs, and more peoples. And they were highly successful at that.

Of course, these Settlers weren't all bad. There was beauty, creativity, and goodness in them. And in their mix were those who questioned the ways of their society. But in the main, these Settlers were an insanely voracious lot, a people who devoured more than they needed and as much as they could get away with.

One day, they "discovered" a valley in the land of Shinar and settled there. Shinar is actually the prairie region of Turtle Island. It wasn't in need of discovering. People had been there forever. But the Settlers didn't care. They pushed them aside and said to each other,

> The flesh of this earth woman is laying waste. Let us rip her up and build fields and farms for ourselves, megafarms 6 x 6 x 6 million acres wide, load them with pesticides and potash, and exhaust a harvest for the cities we are building for ourselves.

And they did it. For themselves.

And then they discovered a network of raging rivers in Turtle Island and said to each other,

> The veins of this earth woman aren't being used to full potential. Let us damn them up, every one, so that we can harness her energy and build a city for ourselves.

And they did it. For themselves.

And then they discovered the boreal forest in Turtle Island and said to each other,

> We must bind this place to our service. Let us remove everything above ground and blast water as hot as hell into the groin of this earth woman; let us get her blood-black gold so we can build cities, banks, and storehouses for ourselves.

And they did it. For themselves.

So the Settlers of Babel built a city and a tower that almost reached heaven. It made them famous. And the corporations and her nation-state were proud. And the military stood on guard to protect it and to ensure the continued intake of civilized resources from uncivilized places. Many of the people were content. Many loved the dream they were living. Many were too distracted by the local sports teams and the latest technologies to question the whole set-up. And some were too beaten down by life — understandably so — to think beyond their lives.

Yet others, they were able. They knew this wasn't working and wouldn't last. They knew something was desperately wrong. The Indigenous were the first. Living in the ghettos, forced away from traditional lands and practices by the violence of progress, they knew that the city's wealth was their poverty. They had been made a national sacrifice "for the greater industrial good." And soon, there were Settlers who were coming to know it too, shaken by the shouts of host peoples, reading the apocalyptic signs of the times. They joined with the Indigenous and prayed for Creator to come down.

Manitou — pity us! God — save us! The powers are united; they're speaking the same language. Can you see what they've done?

Fact. Before the Industrial Revolution, the density of carbon dioxide in the atmosphere, the key cause of global warming, was about 280 parts per million. Today, it has reached 408 parts, far above what's needed to keep global warming at two degrees. And it's still rising, the fastest rise in temperature in the last 10,000 years.

And the people cried, "God damn it!"

Fact. First World countries, which represent less than 20 percent of the world's population, have emitted almost 75 percent of all greenhouse gas pollution that is now destabilizing the climate.

And the people cried, "God damn it!"

Fact. Burn all the oil in Alberta's Tar Sands, the largest industrial project in human history, and we are up to 540 parts per million. Game over planet earth.

And the people cried, "God damn it!"

Fact. The current rate of species extinction is an astonishing 100 to 1,000 times greater than the average extinction rates ever. This means that our culture will destroy one-third to one-half of the planet's species in the next generation. It is the slaughter of the innocents.

And the people cried, "God damn it!"

Fact. Warmer seawater has reduced phytoplankton, the base of the marine food chain, by 40 percent since 1950. Warmer seawater and industrial fishing has reduced the amount of fish in the water by 90 percent since 1850.

And the people cried, "God damn it!"

Fact. The Canadian Government's response to this ecological crisis? Speak fine words about "green growth" and treaty rights, while championing fossil-fuel production by expanding tar sands extraction, twinning pipelines, and whoring itself to the economic gods of capitalism.

And the people cried, "God damn it!"

God damn it indeed.

The powers are in revolt. They don't want to change their ways. "No country will take action on climate change that will hurt its economy," said former Prime Minister Stephen Harper.

¤

In the old story, the Spirit of Yahweh scatters the Settler powers all over the world. In an act of divine grace, the building of that violent city is stopped. We are not there yet. Petropolis is growing rapaciously, and Indigenous lands and lifeforms are suffering inordinately because of it. The powers want to scale the heavens, they want to be gods. And as the Scripture says, "Unless they are stopped, nothing is impossible for them."

But a growing number are coming together. We are watching, talking, strategizing. Hoping against hope, we ponder acts of resistance and survival.

We pray: "Come, Lord! Come Manitou! Scatter the foolishness and dismantle the industrial idols with your love and anger. And do it soon."

And King Melchizedek of Salem brought out bread and wine; he was priest of God Most High. He blessed him and said, "Blessed be Abram by God Most High."

Genesis 14:18–19

THE OATH OF MELCHIZEDEK

Norman Habel

In the Name of El Elyon,
Creator Spirit in the Land of Canaan,
I, Melchizedek,
Canaanite priest of El Elyon
at the sacred shrine of Salem,
hereby swear
that Abraham and I are allies
who have protected this holy land,
that I blessed Abraham in the name of El Elyon,
who, in turn, swore by El Elyon that he would not take
any property of his allies in Canaan.

I also swear by El Elyon
that I welcomed Abraham and his family to this land
and that my people, the Indigenous custodians of Canaan,
have agreed to be joint custodians of this land
with the descendants of Abraham.

I know Canaan is a land of promise,
the land of the Creator Spirit, El,
and I look forward to sustaining this land,
free from colonial invasion,
together with the family of Abraham and
the current families of the land.
May all who hear my voice
respect my oath.

¤

DEAR AUSTRALIAN SETTLERS,

I realize it has been several thousand years since Abraham and I met at Salem and celebrated the blessing of our God, El Elyon. But do you realize that our sacred meeting is wholly relevant for those of you who still claim a connection with Abraham?

First, I am an Indigenous Canaanite priest. My people, the Canaanites, were the Indigenous peoples of the so-called Promised Land. We are the biblical equivalent to the Indigenous peoples of Australia. So I ask you: are you friends with the Indigenous peoples on whose lands you live, as Abraham was? Have you become joint custodians of the land with the Indigenous Australians, just as Abraham did with me and the Indigenous Canaanites?

Second, El Elyon is the Creator Spirit of Canaan, the God of the Indigenous peoples of the land, the God who Abraham recognized and celebrated when he came to Salem. I now ask you: did you acknowledge and honour the Creator Spirit(s) of the Indigenous Australians when you settled in Australia? And if not, are you ready to issue a sacred apology for dismissing the profound faith of Indigenous Australians? A faith that Abraham recognized in Canaan?

Third, the Canaanites were the custodians of Canaan, a land of promise, a people with whom Abraham bonded and made a treaty. Are you aware that you dispossessed Australian custodians in much the same way the Israelites dispossessed my people on the grounds that they had a divine edict to invade the "Promised Land," an edict that negated our covenant relationship with Abraham?

Please friends. Respect my oath, my people, and my God, as Abraham did. Remember the past to live rightly today.

Sincerely,
Melchizedek

When she could hide him no longer she got a papyrus basket for him, and plastered it with bitumen and pitch; she put the child in it and placed it among the reeds on the bank of the river.

Exodus 2:3

I CHOSE MIRIAM

Jennifer Henry

YOU DON'T USUALLY think of this as my story. You don't even know my name. And that's okay if the story is about Miriam — her courage, her leadership, her voice. But my guess is that she is overlooked too, for the men — her hero brother and my villain father. Since I began to open my eyes and ears, I have been turned upside down by what it means to share DNA with those who commit genocide.

There are two things I can't deny. My ancestors sought to destroy Indigenous peoples — out of racial superiority, out of missionary zeal, out of lust for the land, out of illusions of purity. My ancestors. My own father, Pharaoh. My own blood. And I benefit from this terrible legacy. I have privilege I cannot disown. It would be easy to try to do so. I am not the Crown or a man in a man's world — what power do I really have? Yet my lineage, my colour, is royal. I want for little, and my comfort comes from what my Settler ancestors have taken from Indigenous peoples — land, resources, labour. Any child of mine would be safe.

When I met Miriam at the river's edge, it was a moment where I had to make a choice — to collude with my father or strive to ally with the women, Miriam and her mother and Shiprah and Puah, who dared defy him. The story says I took pity. I hope it wasn't that. Yet victim and saviour narratives are so engrained that it could have been. What I hope is that it was simply a human response to injustice — and, most importantly, a saying yes to Miriam who opened a path forward.

There was, of course, nothing simple about it. It was a "No" in the face of genocide. I think I did what I could to stand with one girl, to support one boy, to ally with one family. I recognize that it didn't shake

21

the foundations of my own privilege. And my mind and heart can never, should never, forget the many others, that the genocide goes on. I wasn't brave enough to stand up to all of that.

Looking back, I often wonder if my decision was the right one. Yes, by Miriam's brilliance Moses spent early days in his own family, in his culture and language. But then the only way to ensure his survival was to bring him into my world. To assimilate him.

I should tell you — it would be unfair if I didn't — that I was childless. Did this seem like a solution to soften my own grief, to fill my own emptiness? Did my own needs make me unable to see more systemic possibilities? Did I do what was right for me and call it allyship? Was it the right step in a wrong world or the wrong step in a world that could have been made more right?

I don't regret responding to Miriam, taking her lead, living in that moment by her cue, and not that of my father. It was a small but important rejection of the empire's dictates. And perhaps I used my privilege the best I could. I couldn't do everything, yet I could respond in that moment, in solidarity, and I could begin — a little — to counter the terrible injustices. It felt subversive to draw from the empire's resources to support a mother's care for her own child — a child the empire would have destroyed. No revolution, no Jubilee, but a small symbol, a small conspiracy of hope.

There is so much more I could have done, could do, so much more to be done. It is hard to even imagine a world where Miriam and I live as equals in resources, safety, and opportunity. But it has to be possible. I am nowhere near where I want to be. Narratives of superiority are hard to dislodge from blood and bone, but every day I want to risk, with greater courage, to be part of a radically transformed world.

In the end, when you tell this story, I hope you focus not on the men alone, but on Miriam. Her courage and wisdom opened possibilities towards life when death was at every turn. You need not remember me, but if you do, what's most important is that I chose Miriam. However imperfect, that was a choice for life.

Inspired by Laurel Dykstra's Set Them Free: The Other Side of Exodus.

The cry of the Israelites has now come to me; I have also seen how the Egyptians oppress them. So come, I will send you to Pharaoh to bring my people, the Israelites, out of Egypt.

Exodus 3:9–10

THE FAILED ASSIMILATION OF SAXON

Peter Haresnape

YEARS BACK, WHEN the Queen in England was called Victoria Saxe-Coburg Gotha, a Cree couple gave birth to a son. He was a fine child, a delight to both of them. His mother kept him hidden, fearing that the Royal Canadian Mounted Police (RCMP) would come to take him away to the residential school on the far side of the lake. One day, the RCMP came within sight of their home. In fear of losing him, she strapped the child in her papoose and made for the lake. There, she wrapped him in a blanket and hid him among the wild rice, nestled in an old flour sack. She left his sister to watch over him until the RCMP left.

Meanwhile, the local minister's daughter was passing in a canoe paddled by two of her father's house servants, Cree converts. She had her gun ready, on the lookout for waterfowl. She saw the sack hooked on a half-submerged beech tree and heard the baby crying. She sent one of her bearers to bring it into the canoe and felt sorry when she saw the child. "This is one of the Indian babies," she said, wanting to keep him.

His sister called from the shore, and the bearer translated her question: "Shall I go and get one of the natives to nurse the baby for you?"

"Yes, go!" she answered. So the girl got the baby's mother, and she became his nurse for the years of his infancy. When he was a little older, the minister's daughter came to fetch him to live with her family, and he was baptized Saxon, for as she said, "I found him in a sack — he is the sack's son." He lived with them in the manse attached to the residential school, which the minister ran with an iron fist.

One day, after Saxon had grown older, he went out to the residential school's farm, where he witnessed a teacher savagely beat a young girl for speaking to her sister in Cree. He looked around and waited until the teacher was alone, then killed him with a rock. He dragged the body into the bush and hid it there.

The next day, he went out and witnessed two boys his own age fighting over a hunk of bread. He asked the one grasping it, "Why are you beating another Indian?"

The boy replied, "Who do you think you are, a white man? Are you going to kill me too?" Then Saxon became afraid, because he realized people knew what he had done.

When the minister learned of the missing teacher and heard the rumours that Saxon had been making trouble, he immediately sent for him. Saxon knew that more than one child had died as a result of this man's ministrations, so he fled the manse.

He escaped to an old campsite by Lake Midian. He heard shouting and crept into the bush to witness a team of loggers bullying a group of sisters who had been collecting firewood for their father, a medicine-man they called Jethro. Saxon watched them harassing the women, and then burst out of his hiding place and attacked them until they fled.

Jethro invited Saxon to live with him and work on his trapline. Before long, he was married to one of the old man's daughters, and they had a son together.

In the years that followed, at the residential school where Saxon had grown up, the old minister became obsessed with breaking the children, making them forget the families they had been stolen from. He became meaner than ever, and the children wept bitterly each night as he grew crueller, restricting rations and ordering beatings. They stifled their tears for fear of punishment, but Creator heard their silent sorrow and longing for a comforting mother.

Around this time, Saxon was out on the trapline, far from the campsite of his father-in-law Jethro. He smelt smoke and went to investigate. He saw a bush fire and turned to flee, but became lost and trapped. He was surrounded by the smoke and flames, but the place where he stood did not catch fire.

Surrounded by the fire, he heard a voice: "Saxon, remove your moccasins, for your Creator stands beside you!" The voice continued, "I am the one who has watched you since birth, who cared for your mother, and all her mothers before her. I know your father-in-law, I

25

know this place, and I know you — what you have done, and what you will do."

Saxon hid his face, afraid that he would be punished for the murder he had committed. But the voice persisted, "I've heard the cries of your sisters and brothers, stolen and starved, forced to learn a strange language, taught to farm instead of fish, to fight instead of hunt, and repressed with cruelty and a wicked desire to make them into something that I did not create them to be. So here I am — to bring them out of that place and take them to a rich hunting ground, the place you were taken from, a place where many nations can cohabit. So, go now! I'm sending you to the residential school to bring my people out!"

But Saxon shook his head. "Who do you think I am? A white man? To go and close the school, and bring all those children out? Where would I take them? What would I feed them? This trapline can't support more than my little family."

"I'll be with you," said Creator. "And you don't need to worry about those things. This land is a rich place. You've been taught to fear it, but my friend Jethro has been showing you the good things all around. You are surrounded by life that will sustain you on your journey. You're not a white man, and neither am I. You were raised to follow their ways, to live in their society — but only as an inferior, a servant, a child. They would never have accepted you. So you lashed out the only way you knew, responding with the same fear and violence you had seen all your life. But now, I have found you. I will teach you a new way, and I will go with you."

Then the LORD said to Moses,
"I am going to rain bread from
heaven for you, and each day the
people shall go out and gather
enough for that day. In that way
I will test them, whether they will
follow my instruction or not."

Exodus 16:4

ECONOMIES OF ENOUGH

Carmen Lansdowne

IN THE OLD DAYS, our economies were different. The manna story speaks to me of the strength my Heiltsuk Nation had—how our ancient ways of life naturally aligned to God's created order. Things are different when we believe the world is a place of abundance. If we trust that the Creator has provided us with everything that we might need, there is no need for competition, no need to struggle over scarce resources. We need only take what is required because we trust that there will always be more.

This is the lesson the Israelites had to learn. They doubted that there would be more, but the manna spoiled when they tried to hoard it. They needed to trust that Creator loved them and would provide what they needed. They needed to believe that they should only amass more when it made sense to do so: for rest and to celebrate the rhythms of creation and Creator.

Today, our world is dangerously different. We don't manufacture and prepare food only to meet our needs. In Canada, we collectively throw away almost half of the food that ends up in our homes because it spoils before we can eat it. Food is over-harvested and over-prepared. We manufacture the insatiable desire for that food to drive the engine of our so-called capitalist economy.

This way of life is not consistent with the lessons taught to the Israelites through God's gracious, daily provision of manna and quail, and it is not consistent with Indigenous traditional ways. Those life-ways called us to deep trust and humble "taking." They also called us to "give back." I think of the words of Leanne Betasamosake Simpson

(Mississauga Nishnaabeg) in her article, "Land and Reconciliation: Having the Right Conversations":

> Our nationhood is based on the idea that the earth is our first mother, that "natural resources" are not "natural resources" at all, but gifts from our mother. Our nationhood is based on the foundational concept that we should give up what we can to support the integrity of our homelands for the coming generations. We should give more than we take. It is nationhood based on a series of radiating responsibilities.

Learning when enough is enough is one of our biggest challenges. We have confused our wants for needs. We allow ourselves to be swayed by desire and motivated by fear and greed. We don't stop for rest and sabbath, and in so doing, we forget who we are and whose we are.

What if we dared to return to the old ways? What if we took only what we needed? What if we took care of each other and ensured that all were fed? If we remembered the lessons our grandmothers and grandfathers learned in the desert and in the bush and on the waters?

And you shall hallow the fiftieth year and you shall proclaim liberty throughout the land to all its inhabitants. It shall be a jubilee for you: you shall return, every one of you, to your property and every one of you to your family.

Leviticus 25:10

IN THE SEVENTH ROUND OF
THE 13 MOONS

Rarihokwats

DURING HIS FAST on the most sacred of mountains, a sacred inspiration came to the Elder of the Elders. Speak to your people, say to them:

"Our Mother the Earth must rest from time to time. During the seventh round of the Cycle of the 13 Moons, always give your Mother a rest. During that rest, do not sow your fields. Do not reap what grows and take it to the market. Let your Mother rest. Whatever the Earth your Mother gives, use as food for your family, for yourself, for those who eat at your table. Eat whatever your Mother produces for you. Leave the rest for the Creatures of the Earth, who are also children of your Mother, and so are related to you.

"Count off seven rounds of the seven rounds of the 13 moons. Then count to the 10th day of the seventh moon, and on that day, sound the caracoles everywhere. On that 10th day, give satisfaction, provide reparation for wrong or injury; make amends, accept reconciliation. Consecrate and dedicate this seventh round of the seven rounds of the 13 moons to the proclamation of liberty throughout the land to its entire people. It shall be a jubilee for you; each of you returning to your own homelands, to your own clans, to your own roots.

"Yes, it shall be a jubilee for you. A time not to sow and not to reap what grows of itself, nor to harvest the untended vines. For it is a jubilee and is to be holy for you. Eat only what Creation provides on its land and in its waters. Yes, return to your own roots. Know your own homelands from which you have been made in this Year of Jubilee.

"Make this Jubilee Year a time to avoid taking advantage of others. Follow Creation's original instructions, which were given when you were given life, and you will live safely in the land. Then the land will yield its fruit, and you will eat your fill and live there in safety. You may ask, 'What will we eat in the seventh year if we do not plant or harvest our crops?' You will find that the sixth round of 13 moons will be so bountiful in its gifts that you will prosper also in the seventh round and into the eighth. While you plant during the eighth round, you will eat from the old crop and will continue to eat from it until the harvest of the ninth round of 13 moons comes in.

"The Earth is your Mother. Who would sell their Mother? Remember that you reside on these lands during your time as a visitor, a steward of the land and its gifts, which are intended for your Seventh Generation. The land provides for the life of your children and you must provide for the redemption of the land. If one of your neighbours has needs, you will invite her to your table. You will help her meet her needs. You will expect nothing in return.

"You will tell your neighbour that you want her to continue to be your neighbour and to be in good health. You will not try to make gains at your neighbour's expense. You will not expect your neighbour to return what you have given her. You will not rule over her. You will not consider that she owes you anything.

"Live by these laws of Creation, and every year will be your Jubilee Year."

The land shall not be sold in perpetuity, for the land is mine; with me you are but aliens and tenants. Throughout the land that you hold, you shall provide for the redemption of the land.

Leviticus 25:23–24

NOT YOUR PROMISED LAND

Tamara Shantz

This land is not your retirement plan.
This land belongs to me.

I am disappointed in the Jubilee.

I turn to Leviticus 25
expecting a damning critique
of the colonial enterprise,
our history of conquest.
I anticipate a challenge,
a call to return the land upon which I live
to the Mississaugas, to the Haudenosaunee.

Instead, I discover a scene that is uncomfortably familiar:
This Jubilee, this beautiful ideal,
this law of restoration and redemption
given in a violently taken promised land,
freedom and right of return
only granted to the chosen ones of Israel.

And the original (earlier?) inhabitants are nowhere to be found.

I ponder the Canaanites as I bike past
another condo development,
another restored factory,

this urban scene of restoration and redemption
that I love.

And the original (earlier?) inhabitants are nowhere to be found.

This land is not your retirement plan.
This land was not given to you. This is not your promised land.

It slowly dawns on me.
I am not an Israelite
being challenged to use our given land equitably,
preventing long-term disparity between rich and poor.

It is the Haudenosaunee
who are more akin to that ancient nation,
carrying the heartbeat of Jubilee
alive in their traditional teachings.

This land is not your retirement plan.
This land does not belong to you. You belong to the land.
It is a gift—all things are gift.

I am a foreigner to this teaching,
a newcomer to this place.
I have no capacity to understand
the land as anything but property
to be sold for a profit,
not given, not received.

Liberate me, Great Creator.
The Jubilee has come and gone
and I silently calculate the value of *my* land.

This land is not your retirement plan.

The LORD said to Moses,
"Send men to spy out the
land of Canaan, which I am
giving to the Israelites; from
each of their ancestral tribes
you shall send a man, every
one a leader among them."

Numbers 13:1−2

SCOUTING THE HALDIMAND TRACT

Sara Brubacher

THE COUNCIL MET and talked for many days. Through careful delib-
eration, they discerned a way forward. "Let us send men and women to
scout this land; land that was promised for our use over 200 years ago,
land six miles deep from each side of the Grand River." With approval
from the clan mothers, the idea was brought to the community, who
also agreed.

From each clan and each nation of the Haudenosaunee, men and
women were chosen.

> From the clans of land: bear, wolf, and deer;
> from the clans of water: turtle, eel, and beaver;
> from the clans of air: snipe, hawk, and heron.
> From the nations: Mohawk, Seneca, and Onondaga,
> Cayuga, Oneida, and Tuscarora.

These were their instructions: "Go up and down the river called O:se
Kenhionhata:tie (which in Mohawk means "willow river") and see
what the land is like, and whether the people who live in it are strong
or weak, whether they are few or many, and whether the land they
live in is good or bad, and whether the towns that they live in are un-
walled or fortified, and whether the land is rich or poor, and whether
there are trees in it or not. Be bold, and bring back some of the fruit
of the land."

So the scouts left the Six Nations Reserve, the land in which they
had been living, less than five percent of the land promised them.

They went up the river to its headwaters,
travelling through Brantford and Paris,
Cambridge, Kitchener, and Waterloo,
Elora, Fergus, and Grand Valley,
to its source outside Dundalk.

They also went down the river to its mouth,
through Caledonia and Mount Healy,
Cayuga and Dunnville,
to its mouth at Port Maitland.

At the end of 40 days, they returned from scouting the land. They came to the council and to all the people and showed them the fruit of the land: corn, beans, and squash; BlackBerries and Google Maps. They reported: "We travelled the land that was promised and it is an abundant land; it flows with fish and syrup, and this is its fruit. We found the documents that show how the land was taken from us and the lease money cheated from us. Yet there are many people who live on the land. They have cut the trees and covered the land in boxes. They block the rivers so the fish cannot spawn and bring toxic waste to its headwaters. They are giants on the land with giant machines to tend their crops in straight rows, giant trails to travel quickly in straight lines, giant buildings to reach straight up in the sky."

A woman from the bear clan spoke: "Let us go at once and rejuvenate this land, for we are strong enough. Do we not have proof that the land was set for our use and how it was unlawfully taken from us? Did not some of the people already know that this land was promised to us?"

But others who had gone with her said, "We are not able to go up against these people yet, for they are stronger than us. Their eyes only look at screens and their ears only listen through cords; they will not see or hear us." And so they brought an unfavourable report back to the Haudenosaunee council, saying, "All the people that we saw in it are of great size. To ourselves we seemed insignificant, like grasshoppers, and so we seemed to them."

The LORD spoke to Moses,
saying: Command the Israelites,
and say to them: When you enter
the land of Canaan (this is the
land that shall fall to you for an
inheritance, the land of Canaan,
defined by its boundaries), your
south sector shall extend from the
wilderness of Zin along the side
of Edom. Your southern boundary
shall begin from the end of the
Dead Sea on the east...

Numbers 34:1−3

THE BOUNDARIES AND LIMITS OF SETTLER COLONIALISM

Pekka Pitkänen

I

COMMAND THE EUROPEANS and say to them: When you enter North America, the land that will be allotted to you as an inheritance will have these boundaries:

The Rio Grande will be your southern boundary. The border will then head west, as far as the Pacific Ocean. This Great Sea will be your western boundary.

Your northern boundary will be in the Arctic regions of the American continent.

Your eastern boundary will be the Atlantic Sea.

This will be your land, with its boundaries on every side.

Assign this land as an inheritance for your future states. Thirteen states on the Atlantic seaboard have already received their inheritance, towards the sunrise. It is your manifest destiny.

It is for your government to assist you in apportioning the land as an inheritance for you; your government will settle and divide the land.

II

Command the Germans and say to them: When you enter Poland, Russia, France and beyond, the land that will be allotted to you as an inheritance will have these boundaries:

The Alps will be your southern boundary. The boundary starts from the Caspian Sea and heads towards the Alps. Having passed the Alps the border will head towards the west, onto the Atlantic Sea and across the English Channel.

Your western boundary will be the Atlantic seaboard of the British Isles. The border will then run to the coast of Norway and northwards from there.

Your northern boundary shall be in the Arctic regions of Scandinavia and Russia, all the way to Novaya Zemlya.

Your eastern boundary will start from Novaya Zemlya and run southwards through the Ural Mountains till the Caspian Sea.

This will be your land, with its boundaries on every side.

Assign this land as an inheritance for the Lebensraum of your people, particularly in the East. The people in the core state have already received their inheritance in the centre of Europe.

Your Führer Hitler will lead you in assigning the land as an inheritance for you; your Führer will settle and divide the land.

III

Command the Jews and say to them: When you enter Palestine, the land that will be allotted to you as an inheritance will have these boundaries:

The Gulf of Aqaba will be your southern boundary. The border starts at Eilat and will then head towards the northwest, as far as Gaza and the Great Sea.

Your western boundary will be the Great Sea.

Your northern boundary will start from Nahariyya and head towards the Golan heights and end at Mount Hermon.

Your eastern boundary starts from Mount Hermon and goes down to the slopes east of the Sea of Kinnereth. Then the border will proceed southward along the Jordan till the north end of the Salt Sea. It will then pass through the Salt Sea and from the southern end of the Salt Sea it will proceed southward in the Arabah to Eilat.

This will be your land, with its boundaries on every side.

Assign this land as an inheritance for your future state. You will receive your land little by little. The last parts for you to settle will be the West Bank and the Gaza Strip.

It is for your military leaders to assist you in assigning the land as an inheritance for you; your governments will settle and divide the land.

¤

Visions of territory are central to settler colonialism. And so it comes as no surprise that the promise of land is a key feature in the settler colonial works of Genesis–Joshua. The Israelites, liberated from slavery in Egypt, are to migrate to the land of Canaan, possess it, and enjoy life there (cf. Deuteronomy 8:7–13). Numbers 34 gives a portrayal of the geographical area that the Israelites are to hold for their new life in the promised land (see also Joshua 13–21). In its narrative context, this scripture describes the lay of the land from the vantage of the ancient Israelites at the near beginning of their conquest—when they started settling the Eastern highlands on their way from Egypt to the land of Canaan. The Israelites are to proceed to the land west of the Jordan river from this area of initial settlement and, in the process, Indigenous peoples are to be destroyed (cf. Deuteronomy 7). The legal materials outlined especially in Exodus–Deuteronomy provide a blueprint for the new society that is to be established in the land.

The biblical text provides the reader with an explicitly Israelite vision and point of view. It is a vision, no doubt, that stood at odds with the thinking and perspective of the Indigenous peoples who were in possession of the land, peoples who were sustained and cared for by that "promised land" for generations.

It might seem surprising, even shocking, for readers to realize that the three modern societies re-imagined above also had comparable visions about their own societies. All of them envisaged settler colonial expansion into areas that were held by other peoples. All of them exercised policies and practices of mass dispossession in order to realize their land dreams.

For the U.S. and Canada, the enterprise was successful and Indigenous peoples were subjugated, displaced, and pushed into more or less small and insignificant areas ("reservations" and "reserves") within this territory. For the Germans of the Third Reich, their endeavour was a disastrous failure, resulting in a massive victory by the Russians whom they planned to subjugate and displace. The defeat of the Germans was of course strongly facilitated by the Western allies, including the United States, a country for whom the territorial conquest of Indigenous nations was already close to a century-old at the time.

As concerns modern Israel, immigration to Palestine began in earnest with the formation of Zionism, first concentrating on the west coast of Palestine in the late 19th and early 20th centuries. More territory was annexed, and more Palestinians were displaced with the War of Independence in the 1940s. These events are rightly remembered by Palestinians as the *Nakhba* ("the catastrophe"). The Israeli advance into Palestinian territories continued with the Six Day War in 1967 and, since then, Israel has extended its settlement building in the West Bank, leaving Gaza bereft like an isolated and subjugated native reservation. The similarities to the treatment of Jews in the ghettos of the German empire of the Third Reich scandalize one's mind.

As concerns the biblical texts, even when academics have differing views about how exactly these stories relate to history, they still assert that a new Israelite society was well established in the Canaanite highlands by about the 11th–10th centuries BCE. No doubt, there were areas held by Indigenous peoples that remained to be possessed, with the original inhabitants ultimately being subjugated and assigned to forced labour (Joshua 13:1–6; Judges 1; 19:10–12; 2 Samuel 5:6–9; 1 Kings 9:20–22).

For a range of reasons, many political societies seek to expand their territories and jurisdiction. Unfortunately, the perspective and benefits of the expanding society are not often congruent with those of the peoples and societies that are being expanded on. Today, all peoples are directly or indirectly affected and shaped by the policies, practices, and rhetorics of the most dominant expanding society the world has ever known—the United States of America. In addition to its hegemonic ideological, political, and economic power, the U.S. has a controlling military presence—some 800 military bases—in more than 70 countries in the world, including Israel. The American empire is clearly a settler colonial power, with what appears to be an insatiable desire to expand its influence and control across the world. Its view of expansion, often clothed in a seemingly innocent garb of "global freedom and democracy," is a view cast from a position of power. But one does not need to assume that "might" makes "right."

To cultivate peace and justice between societies and nations, it is apparent that there is no room for the logics and practices of settler colonial dispossession. And to undo the harms wrought by such devastating logics and practices, it's clear that this would involve, at the very least, an admission of past wrongdoings together with a restoration of life and health to the impacted peoples—a restoration that would include property and traditional lands and territories.

While there are examples of decolonization in recent history, including Algeria with the French, Korea with the Japanese, and Eastern Europe with the Germans, these were achieved in the cauldron of war. The settler societies in those lands were not actively supporting Indigenous calls for decolonization, restoration, and reparation. In settler colonialism, there is no "invisible hand" operating for the good of all. Instead, there is a hand of destruction at work in a zero-sum game. Accordingly, alternative modes of thinking and living together are required, modes that can help all of us move beyond the totalizing capitalism and neo-liberalism that are so much a part of today's settler colonial realities.

One gift that could help in mapping out such a future, offering us boundaries of respect and principles of repair, is the *United Nations Declaration on the Rights of Indigenous Peoples*. *The Declaration* is a short proclamation that sets forth the "minimum standards for the survival, dignity, and well-being of the Indigenous peoples of the world" (Article 43). Crafted by Indigenous and State representatives over the span of two decades, *The Declaration* stands today as a global human rights instrument that can guide states and settler societies in their efforts to mend significant historic injustices and reject present colonialism. But it will take people, like you and me, to make that happen. We may be reminded of what the black freedom fighter, Frederick Douglass, once said: "Power never concedes nothing without a demand. It never did. It never will." If so, if we do not quietly submit, but persist in resisting injustice, perhaps humankind can still have cause for hope, improving life on the planet we occupy. Land is a central and vital resource for a wholesome and prosperous existence for all, not just for some.

Moses convened all Israel, and said to them: Hear, O Israel, the statutes and ordinances that I am addressing to you today; you shall learn them and observe them diligently.

Deuteronomy 5:1

THE 15 COMMANDMENTS

Musa W. Dube

HEAR, O CREATION COMMUNITY, the decrees and laws God declares in your hearing today. Learn them and be sure to follow them. In the 21st century, in the post-colonial era, in the neo-liberal era, and the eras of global warming and climate change, the Creator God made a covenant with all members of the Earth Community, saying, "I am the God who created the Universe and the Earth and everything in it. I created them good, beautiful, interconnected, and perfect. Therefore:

COMMANDMENT 1: You shall recognize the Divine Spirit in all creation, in the various forms of its manifestation in different cultures, and among all members of the Earth Community.

COMMANDMENT 2: You shall recognize the image of God in all members of the Creation Community. My Spirit was already hovering over the Earth while it was still dark and formless. Then I created all things in the Creation Community, both animate and inanimate, through my divine Word and Spirit. I also created all human beings, in their differences, in my image. Therefore, all members of the Creation Community are made in my own image.

COMMANDMENT 3: You shall not misuse any member of the Creation Community, animate or inanimate. The Creator God will not hold anyone guiltless who misuses and abuses God's Creation Community.

COMMANDMENT 4: Observe the Sabbath day by keeping it holy as the Creator God has commanded you. Six days you shall labour and do all your work, but the seventh day is a Sabbath to the Creator God. On it you shall not do any work. All your machines used for cooking, cooling, industry, transport, and farming shall be shut down to allow the Earth to rest from pollution. Any systems of any form that emit pollutant gases into the atmosphere shall stop and rest.

On the Sabbath, you shall not do any work, neither you, nor your daughter or son, nor your female or male or intersex labourers, nor your ox, your donkey, or any of your domestic animals, nor any foreigners residing in your villages and towns, so that female and male and intersex labourers may rest as you do. Remember that God created all members of the Creation Community and made them very good. You are to keep the whole Creation Community holy, avoiding all forms of pollution and giving the whole Creation Community the opportunity to replenish itself to its original goodness. Observe the Sabbath day.

COMMANDMENT 5: Honour your parents as the Creator your God has commanded you, so that you may live long and that it may go well with you in the land into which the Creator God has welcomed you.

COMMANDMENT 6: You shall not murder. You shall not murder either directly or indirectly. You shall not murder by poisoning the waters of the Earth or the food chain through introducing pollutants into the streams, rivers, lakes, and oceans, leading to the proliferation of life-threatening diseases. You shall not murder by introducing destructive and life-threatening pollutants in the air. You shall not murder by practising exploitative economic and political systems that nurture poverty and lead to the sickness and death of members of the Creation Community. You shall not murder by engaging in civil, regional, or worldwide wars that claim millions of lives. You shall not murder any member of the Creation Community, for all life is sacred to me, the Creator God.

COMMANDMENT 7: You shall not commit infidelity of any form to your sexual partner.

COMMANDMENT 8: You shall not steal. You shall not steal directly or indirectly as individuals or through systems and structures, from individuals or communities. You shall not steal from God the Creator through greed and the exploitation of the Earth's resources, leading to the destruction of the Earth and the impoverishment of millions of members of the Creation Community. You shall not steal by practising the idolatrous ways of imperialism, colonization, capitalism, neo-capitalism, and neo-liberal economics, which exploit and dispossess what is rightfully due to billions of people. You shall not steal from Indigenous communities by appropriating their resources and knowledge through unfair and non-reciprocal trade of goods and ideas. You shall not steal from women, workers, economic refugees, and other minorities by not paying for their labour, and by not paying a living wage. You shall not steal the lives of people through human trafficking, or prey on economically-challenged families, countries, and regions.

COMMANDMENT 9: You shall not give false testimony against your neighbour directly or indirectly, as individuals or through systems and structures. You shall not give false testimony against your neighbour by writing their histories, stories, cultures, and religions to suit your needs, to subjugate them, or to legitimize their oppression.

COMMANDMENT 10: You shall not be covetous towards your neighbour. You shall not covet your neighbour's partner. You shall not set your desire on your neighbour's country, house, field, domestic animals, business, their female or male or intersex worker, or anything that belongs to them.

COMMANDMENT 11: You shall not exploit minorities among you. I am the Creator God, who created all people in my own image. You shall not oppress, exploit, or dispossess widows, orphans, and strangers among you on the basis of their vulnerability. You shall not oppress, exploit, or dispossess women on their basis of their gender. You shall not oppress, exploit, or dispossess people of colour on the basis of their race. You shall not oppress, exploit, or dispossess ethnic minorities on the basis of their cultures and beliefs. You shall not oppress, exploit, or dispossess sexual minorities on the basis of their sexual orientation. You shall not oppress, exploit, or dispossess people with physical challenges on the basis of their disability. You shall not oppress, exploit, or dispossess children or senior citizens on the basis of their age. You shall not oppress, exploit, or dispossess people who are ill with any disease on the basis of their health, for I am the Creator God who created all people in my own image.

COMMANDMENT 12: You shall not practice any form of slavery. I am the Creator God who created all human beings in my own image and I am the liberator God who brought the Israelites out of Egypt, out of the house of slavery. Therefore, you shall not enslave any person, be it on the basis of class, race, caste, gender, citizenship, or any other socially constructed category or vulnerability.

COMMANDMENT 13: You shall not abuse, exploit, or oppress any animal in the more-than-human world. I am the Creator God who created all animals on Earth.

COMMANDMENT 14: You shall not abuse, exploit, or oppress the Earth, for the Earth and everything in it belongs to me.

COMMANDMENT 15: You shall love the Creator God with all your heart, soul, and strength. I am the Creator God, who created the Universe, the Earth, and everything in it. I created all things in perfection, goodness, interconnection, and beauty. I created all things in my Word, and my Spirit remains in the Creation Community. I created all people in my image. Therefore, you shall love and worship the Creator God by keeping the whole creation sacred, observing all these commandments in your families, workplace, communities, countries, regions, continents, and throughout the Earth as a whole.

These are the commandments that the Creator God proclaimed in a thunderous voice, not from some high mountain, but from the tips of breaking, melting glaciers. God proclaimed them before the whole Creation Community, and God added nothing more. Then God wrote them on three stone tablets and gave them to the Earth Community.

When the LORD your God brings you into the land that you are about to enter and occupy, and he clears away many nations before you — the Hittites, the Girgashites, the Amorites, the Canaanites, the Perizzites, the Hivites, and the Jebusites, seven nations mightier and more numerous than you — and when the LORD your God gives them over to you and you defeat them, then you must utterly destroy them. Make no covenant with them and show them no mercy.

Deuteronomy 7:1–2

DESTROY EVERYTHING

Derrick Jensen

WHEN THE LORD your God—sometimes called God, sometimes Empire, sometimes Settler Society, sometimes Civilization—brings you into the land that you are about to enter and occupy, and he clears away many nations before you—the Taino, Beothuk, Chimariko, Koroa, Timucua, Hillibee—and all the other nations more numerous than you; and when the Lord your God—sometimes called Soldiers, sometimes Priests, sometimes Settlers—gives them over to you and you defeat them, then you must utterly destroy them. Make no treaty with them— at least no treaty you will honour—and show them no mercy. Take their daughters and sons for your boarding schools, for that will turn away their children from following their own gods, their own religions, their own ways of life. None of these children must be allowed to escape. If they do, then the anger of the Lord will be kindled against you, and he will destroy you quickly.

So this is how you must deal with them: demolish their homes, dam their rivers, dig up their mountains, hew down their forests, and destroy everything they hold sacred. For you are a people holy to the Lord your God—sometimes called Progress, sometimes called Technology—and the Lord your God has chosen you out of all the peoples on Earth to be his people, his treasured possession. (Or maybe you just chose yourself and told yourself God said it.) The Lord did not set his heart on you and choose you because you were more numerous than any other people—for you were the least of all peoples. It was because the Lord loved you and kept the oath that he swore to your ancestors, that the Lord has brought you out with a mighty hand,

and redeemed you from slavery to Nature, and instead made Nature your slave.

Know therefore that the Lord your God is God, the faithful God who maintains covenant loyalty with those who love him and keep his commandments, to 1,000 generations; the God who doesn't delay, but repays in their own person those who reject him. Therefore, observe diligently the commandment—to enslave all of life—that the Lord is commanding you today.

¤

If you heed this commandment, by enslaving all there is, the Lord your God will maintain with you the covenant loyalty that he swore to your ancestors: he will love you, bless you, and multiply you; he will bless the fruit of your womb and the fruit of your ground; your grain and your wine and your oil; the increase of your cattle and the issue of your flock; your machines and your stock markets; your tanks and guns and airplanes; your jails and prisons; your shopping malls and parking lots; your monocrops and factory farms; your blasted streams and denuded hillsides; your empty skies and silent springs. You shall be the most blessed of peoples, with neither sterility nor barrenness among you or your livestock, and with cable, phone, and high-speed internet to secure all your needs in this brave new world.

The Lord will turn away from you every illness; all the dread diseases of Nature that you experienced, he will not inflict on you, but he will lay them on all who hate you. They will die of smallpox and mumps and measles. They will die of chytrid and white nose syndrome. They will die by the sword and by the bullet. They will die by the drugs and alcohol you first give, then sell, to them. You shall devour all the peoples that the Lord your God is giving over to you, showing them no pity; you shall not serve their gods, for that would be a snare to you. You shall not love them. You shall not love the land. You shall not love this world.

If you say to yourself, "These nations are more numerous than I; how can I dispossess them?" do not be afraid of them. Just remember what the Lord your God—sometimes called Civilization, sometime Empire, sometimes Science, sometimes Capitalism, always in truth being Conquest—did to the rest of the world. How the Lord your God destroyed the forests of the Garden of Eden, the headwaters of the Pishon, Gihon, the Tigris, and the Euphrates. How he cut down the cedars of Lebanon, the trees of Greece and Italy, the forests of North Africa. How he made it so forests precede you and deserts dog your heels. How he destroyed every wild and fecund and alive place you settled.

Remember how the Lord your God — sometimes called Progress — drove before him the creatures of the land and the humans of the land who were not his Chosen People. Remember the signs and wonders, the mighty hand and the outstretched arm by which the Lord your God — sometimes called Technology, sometimes the Application of Organized Violence — made you master of the world. The Lord your God will help you destroy all the peoples of whom you are afraid. Moreover, the Lord your God will send the pestilence against them, until even the survivors and the fugitives are destroyed. Have no dread of them, for the Lord your God, who is present with you, is a great and awesome God.

The Lord your God will clear away these nations before you little by little; you will not be able to make a quick end of them, otherwise the wild animals will become too numerous for you. And you don't want to share a world with wild animals. This is why the Lord told you to utterly destroy the flocks of passenger pigeons so large they darkened the sky for days at a time, told you to kill 60 million buffalo, told you to kill the prairie dogs, the salmon, the lampreys, wolves, grizzly bears, Eskimo curlews. (Or maybe you just told yourself to do it and then told yourself God told you to do it.) But the Lord your God will give them over to you and throw them into great panic, until they are destroyed. He will hand their kings over to you, and you shall blot out their name from under heaven; you will destroy them, you will destroy every Indigenous nation, you will destroy every living being, you will destroy all Nature, you will destroy everything, for the Lord is a jealous God, who hates all of the world — except you. No one will be able to stand against you.

You shall burn with fire the forests they consider sacred, the forests they call home. You shall plow the prairies and drain the marshlands. You shall dam the rivers and remove the mountaintops and fill the oceans with oil and plastic. Do not covet the beauty of the world, of the land or the ocean or the air or anyone who lives in these, because you could be ensnared by this beauty; it is abhorrent to the Lord your God. Do not bring an abhorrent thing like Nature into your heart, or you will be set apart for destruction like it. You must utterly detest and abhor it, for it is set apart for destruction.

The LORD said to Joshua, "See, I have handed Jericho over to you, along with its king and soldiers. You shall march around the city, all the warriors circling the city once. Thus you shall do for six days."

Joshua 6:2–3

TO THE PRESENT DAY

Daniel Hawk

THE PURITAN COLONISTS, who passed through the waters and entered Algonquin lands, arrived with a fierce determination to establish a new community that manifested the ordering ideals bestowed by their God. They saw, in those who inhabited the land, savage and lawless peoples devoid of moral sensibility and bound by Satan. This savage presence had to be erased. Only then could the land be remade into a place where God's glory settled, and God's people could become a city set on a hill.

At first, the colonists needed help and protection. As in the biblical story of Joshua, they found helpers like Rahab, who befriended and sheltered them. Then, like Israel at Gilgal, they renewed and consecrated themselves for their errand into the wilderness. The Puritans initially favoured benign interaction with the more powerful peoples who surrounded them, but when the Pequots resisted colonial expansion, the impulse of violent erasure flared up with a vengeance. Echoing Israel's conquest at Jericho, the Puritans launched a pre-emptive strike against a village on the Mystic River. They showed no mercy.

After being repulsed, the Puritan force surrounded the palisade, set the town on fire, and killed everyone attempting to escape, more than 500 children, women, and men. A campaign ensued, which saw massacres at two more villages and ended only when the Pequots were wiped out.

The Pequot War (1636–38) proved to be the first of many that mimicked Israel's campaigns of conquest. As the United States expanded westward, the new nation wove the conquests of Indigenous peoples into a narrative that cast the Settlers as an invincible force propelled by a transcendent destiny, blessed by God to clear the land. The narrative celebrated the winning of the West in the triumphal cadences of Joshua, even as the New Israel replicated biblical Israel's program of subjugation and removal in the belief that, in the picturesque words of Oliver Wendell Holmes, the "red crayon sketch" would be rubbed out and "the canvas made ready for a picture of manhood a little more like God's own image."

The biblical story of Jericho is all about Israel and all about God—their victory and their destruction, their power and their glory—save for a brief note that Rahab and her family have lived within Israel to the present day. "To the present day" voices the startling admission that the invaders' program of erasure did not succeed. Rahab and her family do not only inhabit the nation's past but the nation's present as well. Rahab and her family remain in the land and retain their identity, set outside the camp by the conquerors, yet living within the nation that occupies the land of her ancestors. The note, and others like it in Joshua, blunts the impulse to situate the peoples of the land within Israel's past and pointedly renders them present and visible.

In the United States, Indigenous peoples resist the same impulse by their presence in the land to this present day. Though rendered largely invisible by a mainstream gaze that sees them only as figures in the nation's past, they too remain. Despite wars, massacres, epidemics, and removals, having endured waves of civilizing projects, pacification policies, boarding schools, tribal termination programs, thefts of land, resources, and trust funds, relocations, forced adoptions, harassment, and insults, they have survived to the present day. The Indigenous peoples of the United States remain a presence in the land, speaking the failure of the program to erase them by violence and assimilation, honouring ancestral attachments to the land, and contesting the American myth of civilized superiority.

So he told her his whole secret, and said to her, "A razor has never come upon my head; for I have been a nazirite to God from my mother's womb. If my head were shaved, then my strength would leave me; I would become weak, and be like anyone else."

Judges 16:17

HEROES SAVE LIVES

Tobin Miller Shearer

THEY SAY HE was a hero. And, yes, I mourned his passing. I had loved the man. But heroes save lives, don't they? This man never did.

I remember when I first heard of him. My neighbour was grieving the loss of her family. Her father, brother, husband, sons—all killed by a bloody baseball bat wielded by some dread-locked white man on a berserker rampage. She didn't know his name when I first saw her, or she was too overwhelmed with grief to say his name out loud. But others made sure that I knew.

With time, I heard all the tales. The grizzly torn in two. The 30 tribal kinsmen slain for their powwow regalia in bloody fulfillment of a wager at his stillborn wedding. The casinos and timber forests burned by pairs of mule deer, their tails bound to flaming torches. The many more Flathead members he beat to death in retaliation for the murder of his would-be father-in-law and would-have-been wife.

Even my people told the stories with awe. Some of them expressed their respect for these warrior ways. But he bore the stink of death. That I remember all too well, for we spent much time in the close quarters of my home.

We met by chance. Only that morning I had heard yet another tale of his strength, that he had toppled the Ronan arch, chained it to his 4 x 4, and dragged it up the Mission Mountains, defiling our sacred space as he climbed. Those who had gathered to escort him off the reservation stood silent, stunned, immobile by the twisted wreckage he had left behind. Typical of the man. Always over the top. He humiliated an entire town and with it, our nation as a whole.

60

I met him the morning after this purported feat but did not know who he was. He had driven up to Dayton, where I have always lived and always will, to fish on the Flathead Lake. The fishing here is good.

I remember his self-satisfied grin. Not a care in the world. We talked. The next morning, he left in broad daylight. My neighbours saw him leave. That was all it took. By that evening, delegates from the tribal council, leaders whom I respected, men intent only on protecting our people from the marauder who had come wandering into our home, reminded me who I was, recalled to me the land I stood on, and informed me of this white man's violence, of the thousands dead at his hand. They told me the name of the man who had spent the night under my roof and in my bed.

I was afraid. I knew he would be back. I knew the violence of which he was capable. I agreed to find the source of his strength. The money they gave was of far less importance than that he be stopped, that he not add any others to his murder count. Too many of us had been killed already.

You know the story of what happened. How he tricked me with claims that handcuffs, nylon ropes, or rubber bands in his hair would sap his strength. How I grew ever more determined to never see another woman widowed by the violence of his hand. How I asked and asked again. And how I just kept asking.

Finally he answered. And so I cut his hair.

Years later — after they had rebuilt the community centre, restored the pine log beams, and elected new officials to take the place of the tribal leaders he had murdered in his final act of blinded rage — I was reading on my porch when my neighbour sat down beside me. We were both old women then. Both without children. Both alone save for each other and the memories we carried.

She asked me, "Would you do anything differently?"

I stared at the cover of my book and thought of the man who had shared my bed, of the stories they still told around me, just outside my hearing, of the strands of his hair in my hands. And I thought of what it meant to be a hero. But I did not respond. I did not speak his name. And so she sat with me without speaking. And we sat some more.

So she said, "See, your sister-in-law has gone back to her people and to her gods; return after your sister-in-law." But Ruth said, "Do not press me to leave you or to turn back from following you! Where you go, I will go; where you lodge, I will lodge; your people shall be my people, and your God my God."

Ruth 1:15–16

WHAT ABOUT ORPAH?

Vivian Ketchum

IT IS 1936. I live near the Red River in Winnipeg. I am a brown woman looking for safety in a land that's fast becoming white. After residential school, I married into a mining family, married a handsome husband, married a white Christian man. I was poor and they were wealthy—until sorrow came upon our doorsteps. Like a cold wind sweeping through a tent, tuberculosis took most of our family. Including my husband.

My mother in-law begged me to leave her and to return to my Indian home in the Northwest Territories. Dene land. I refused.

"Your path is my path. Your ways are now my ways," I tell my mother-in-law. "I will walk with you until the day I die."

Why should I return to a land that's a stranger to me? I've lost the language of my people. Lost the customs. Lost the traditions. The old prayers are but a fading memory. I now pray to a new God. The real God. The one—I've been told over and over again—and only God.

My sister Orpah has kissed us goodbye. She's returning to her land and to her heathen traditions. My heart breaks. Isn't she afraid of being an outsider in her homeland? She's been away too long! How will they welcome her with her foreign ways? I pity her. And I'm sad that's she's going back to those pagan ways.

And yet, I admire her. Even respect her.

As for me, I'll walk forward with Naomi, my mother-in-law, in this new land that promises prosperity. It is easier to walk with her than to return with my sister and struggle to pick up the traditions of my people. I will wear the clothes and ways of a different family. For I belong neither here nor there.

If I follow my white mother in her land, there's more certainty, even the promise of riches and perhaps a husband once more. Yes, I admit it. I'll forsake traditional ways for security. I am not strong like Orpah. My sister's path is unsure. When she returns to our homeland, they may not welcome her.

I will follow and even be buried in the manner of my mother's people. Their roof will be mine.

I know that I'll give up a large part of myself in doing this; that I could actually find myself if I decided to follow my sister, Orpah, to our homeland. But how can I? It's not realistic. I am only a brown woman in a white stranger's new-found land.

But the people refused to listen to the voice of Samuel; they said, "No! but we are determined to have a king over us, so that we also may be like other nations, and that our king may govern us and go out before us and fight our battles."

1 Samuel 8:19 – 20

GIVE US A KING

Deanna Zantingh

Don't fool yourself.
Despite potential for
wealth, titles, and other securities,
we humans are fragile clay jars.
Consider Israel's great turn,
the anxious clutch of
the commonweal through crown
and monarchy.

In those days, Samuel's sons ruled:
Joel, meaning "Yahweh is God" (power)
and Abijah, meaning "Yahweh is my father" (relation),
but they ruled with corruption and greed.
Joel lived like "Joel is God"
and Abijah lived like
"Yahweh is not my neighbour's father."
Distorted power and relation,
cyclical and typical
of our own time and place,
and then the people demand a king.

Crying out for a king is not
merely poor seeing,
it's not even closed eyes.
It's like forgetting one has eyes at all.

This earth is everyone's home.
All the great mystics and spiritual teachers
have wagered their lives on this:
Prayer is awareness of one's world;
Prayer is awareness of something or someone else in one's world;
Prayer is awareness it isn't one's world at all;
Prayer is awareness that there is only one world
and this one world is everyone's home.

And in the streets,
I can still hear cries for a king,
for someone to guarantee security,
for someone to take away our fear.
"We want to be like the nations."

It is fear that has clawed at the earth
and clawed at bodies in colonial Canada.
If you have power,
you can control.
If you can control,
you will have security.
If you are secure,
you will be comfortable,
and in your comfort,
you will be
the ultimate
reality.

You are a fragile clay jar.

No amount of security
can hold your fear at bay.
You will always feel threatened by
those with the ability to unite us.

The only thing that can break you free
from this prison of fear

is prayer,
the kind that opens your world
and brings the love at the foundation of the earth
to full completion within you.
There can be no peace, no security,
if we cannot first learn
to find it within.

Dear world,
don't run from the claws of one animal
into the snare of another
as though you have no eyes.
Corrupt kings will make you forget
what corrupt local leaders remind you:
this earth is your health
and, in the end,
it is an illusion to believe
you can own it, divide it, or reshape it.
And though my ears are ringing and
I'm getting a headache
from the patriarchal babble
my spirit resonates with those jazz blues,
drum beats, heart beats,
cries of all the coloured bodies,
beauty of all the unity this universe has to offer.

All we need is gifted all around us.
All the great mystics, spiritual teachers,
dancing sisters, and drumming kokums
have wagered their lives on this.
Bathed in prayer and sacred water,
don't feed the desire for security.
Expose its false foundation,
transform it to unity.

True power is to access the spiritual,
to look around and listen,

to be connected with others
and put them first,
connecting with the Spirit
you may not even know is moving you.

We all have eyes. Open yours
to the gift of grace in the whole of the universe.
We're drowning in the grace of interconnectedness
while living like we have no eyes to see it.

The unity of the world
offers itself to each of us.

Sisters and brothers,
no matter your pain,
the things you have endured or inflicted,
the dehumanization you have suffered or caused,
the fear and insecurity you have felt,
the scars on land and body,
you are never beyond being moved by the Spirit
never beyond remembering you have eyes,
never beyond a clay jar filled with love and beauty.

True power is knowing this for oneself
and awaking to
all of the world in this light.
This earth is everyone's home,
Don't fool yourself.

Then David's anger was greatly
kindled against the man. He said
to Nathan, "As the LORD lives, the
man who has done this deserves
to die; he shall restore the lamb
fourfold, because he did this thing,
and because he had no pity."

2 Samuel 12:5–6

THE STORYTELLER'S REBELLION

Bob Haverluck

IN THE SPRING of the year when kings go to make war, King David remained in Jerusalem. He made war there. But in his early days, David hadn't been a warrior. He had been peace itself. A shepherd who led his sheep to green pastures and to lie down beside still waters. A songbird, a singer of songs that restored downcast spirits. Even the ever-sad King, the down-in-the-dumps Saul, was up and dancing when the shepherd boy's music got into his ears.

But a day came when Philistine soldiers invaded the land with their champion Goliath. That day, the shepherd boy put down his shepherd's crook and harp. Picked up his slingshot and one stone. And David sent that stone singing through the air, making a third eye between Goliath's other two. War game over: trophy to Israel's Rock Star. For a while, a kind of peace.

Eventually, however, the insecure King Saul exiled the popular giant-killer David. More survivor than songster, David fled. Soon, David-the-exile sought shelter from the Philistine king, becoming their new Goliath. Famously murdering men and women without mercy, David lived like a man with no relatives. To his new Philistine protectors, David brought a booty of sheep, cattle, oxen... even while planning their defeat.

In time, David became Israel's king. The poet Samuel had warned about KINGS. Kings are Egypt's Pharaohs all over again, he said. Kings promised security without end, but the cost of having kings would be terrible. More and more of the world that the people loved would be taken to feed the ever-swelling appetite of kings and their princes. Having enough, the king would want more, hungering for a bigger army, palace, and temple. The people, forests, animals, rivers, and the earth would become the supper of kings. Kings of Israel no less than the kings of Babylon.

So in the spring of the year when kings go to make war, King David remained in Jerusalem and added Bathsheba to his many wives. And her husband was added to the dead. But nothing was said. Nothing was spoken. It seemed that this presidential manoeuvre had gone unnoticed. Until Nathan, the poet nephew of the alarm-bell Samuel, came to the king's door.

The poet was trembling with uncertainty. For days he had brooded, "How can I get the king to listen, to hear, really hear the bad news? Plain speaking won't work. Might a song help truth be heard? David is big on songs. However, I am no singer…Maybe a story? A parable dropped into the king's earhole could do the necessary mischief."

Nathan was invited into the palace and was seated across from the king, who wisely was suspicious of the prophet poet's visit. "I have brought you a little story," the visitor began. "The story is of another time than now, somewhere else than here…a sort of parable."

"Ahh, not a true story then," said the king, relaxing into his comfy chair, ready to listen.

"Once there was a very poor farmer who had but one ewe lamb," began the poet. "This was the only lamb he owned. On the cold nights, he would keep the lamb warm against his breast. During the day, the poor farmer's children helped the lamb grow full bodied and strong, bringing her juicy grass and clover. Now, when the poor farmer and family dreamed their dreams, they dreamed of the ewe surrounded by a field of her lambs peacefully grazing."

The king mused, "What a sweet story this is."

The poet continued, "One day, a great land owner and his men on tall horses came riding into the poor man's yard. 'What a fine lamb you have there,' declared the rich man to the poor man. 'What an excellent shepherd you must be.'"

Sensing the worst, the poor man dared speak, "She is my only lamb, your honour. My children's future is carried in her."

"Yes, yes," yawned the great land owner. "I love children. Especially poor children. But tomorrow, I have guests arriving and does not God demand hospitality? You do believe in God, don't you? I am a great believer myself, if I may say so. Born many times over. So in God's holy name, I order my men to take that lamb, cut its throat, and bring her carcass home to my kitchen. Besides, the lamb is not really your lamb, is she? She's God's lamb. And to God she shall be returned. Amen."

And with the dead lamb, the rich man and followers rode away.

King David, unable to contain himself, roared, "That man is a swine and ought to be hanged!"

"The poor man?" asked the poet.

"No, no, the rich man!" replied the king.

The poet then whispered to his highness, "YOU are that man."

And King David became silence itself.

Silent, David sat remembering that he had once been a shepherd with a true shepherd's heart. Attentive, tending tenderly to the sheep. Content with such gentleness. Now, those nearby called him a Shepherd King. But in the silence, he was given to know that he had become more king than shepherd. And he who had forgotten how to blush, blushed. Not with a shame that ends in guilt. But with a wise guilt that begins a turning. And so King David was given to turn, turn, turn and to begin, begin again.

There is no record of the poet Nathan telling any more parables. But there was a later poet who became well known as a teller of many parables that turned listeners from nowhere to here, from another time to their blessed, yet broken time.

Naboth the Jezreelite had a vineyard in Jezreel, beside the palace of King Ahab of Samaria. And Ahab said to Naboth, "Give me your vineyard, so that I may have it for a vegetable garden, because it is near my house; I will give you a better vineyard for it; or, if it seems good to you, I will give you its value in money."

1 Kings 21:1–2

THE LAND: OUR LIFE

Ellen F. Davis

Naboth the small farmer, as he is led out to his death:

Ahab tried to make a deal with me about Daddy and Granddaddy's land. I could hardly believe my ears. The king of Israel wanted to buy land I could not sell, and he could never own — was he crazy or just stupid? It's my ancestral inheritance! God's trust to this family, generation to generation! Ahab called it a mere "field."

It would be blasphemy for me to sell that land, I told him. It was God's own truth. Treating farmland like real estate, putting a price on it — I'd sell my own body before I would sell my people off this land.

They meant to tell a lie, those talking snakes with their trumped-up charge against me. But God took their coiling words and twisted them into a strange kind of truth.

"Naboth blessed our God and king!"

That's what they said in Jezebel's kangaroo court. It's a local expression. A winking way of saying I cursed. But I was the only one in court today who really did bless God and king. By refusing to sell my land to Ahab, I recognized God as the Creator of this good land who lets every small farmer live on it and care for it, in good faith. By refusing to sell my land, I recognized the responsibility of the king, that God expects political powers to stand up for Torah, for a God-given vision of community, with humans, animals, and land flourishing together. Yet these royals couldn't care less. They honour only their short-term interests.

I'll die today. But trust me. Ahab's house won't last long. He's the one who's sold off his heritage and trust from God.

1 Kings 21

Elijah the prophet, speaking to Ahab and to the "rulers" of the 21st century:

You fraud, Ahab! Your rhetoric about having a garden next to the palace was nothing but political spin. You wanted the valuable wine from Naboth's ancestral vineyard to flow into the royal revenue stream, to support your big standing army, to prop up your aggressive military agenda. To get that, you attacked Israel's ancient understanding of community, Israel's belief in shared power based on land tenure for all. You knew full well—people, land, and God are bound together. How could you betray that? Religion, economics, and land care are inextricably intertwined! Naboth knew that! And he knew that Israel's king could never legitimately be a power grabber, as in other nations. Threatened by that knowledge, you and Jezebel defamed and murdered him. For this, your royal house will fall.

And now, you rulers of the earth in this 21st century, wise up (Psalm 2:10)! Recognize your Ahab ways! Do you know—of course you do!—that right now, six corporations that control industrial agriculture around the world are anticipating approval from the United States government for the biggest agribusiness merger in history? They're consolidating their "royal" shares of the global seed and pesticide markets. Industrial agriculture is violently defaming God's trust! It's murdering the land! Can't you see it? Industrial agriculture is a major driver of fossil fuel consumption, greenhouse gas emissions, and global warming; it's the chief cause of large-scale deforestation, soil degradation, water degradation, and rural poverty around the world; it produces lower yields and higher costs for farmers than any ecological farming methods—yet less than two percent of the United States Agriculture budget goes into agroecological research. This royal business will fall, and soon!

The cultural paradigm is shifting. Communities around the world— rural and urban, Indigenous and Settler—are re-membering themselves and the land. Science, tradition, faith, and economics are aligned in the practice of agriculture that works not like a conveyor belt, but an ecosystem. God remembers the land (Leviticus 26:42). Will you?

Shaphan the secretary informed the king, "The priest Hilkiah has given me a book." Shaphan then read it aloud to the king. When the king heard the words of the book of the law, he tore his clothes.

2 Kings 22:10–11

LOST AND FOUND

Steve Heinrichs

IT'S THE YEAR 2030, and everything is about to change. She is the youngest prime minister to ever take office. She is 38 years old, and she will serve for eight years. Her dad is from British Columbia, her mom from Prince Edward Island. And she does her best to do what is right.

In the third year of the prime minister's term, Ottawa is experiencing significant struggle with host peoples; grassroots are demonstrating, elders are crying out, and many are publicly fasting in the streets. They are talking about broken covenants. They are proclaiming "Treaty rights!" The prime minister is confused. "Why are they so frustrated? Why all the protest?"

The Department of Indigenous Affairs tells her to ignore it. "They already get more than they deserve." "They're blowing off steam. It'll pass." But the prime minister decides otherwise, decides to do some homework. She summons a trusted secretary, "Go to the federal archives, and go to the people. See what you can find."

And that's when they find it. The Treaty of Niagara, 1764.

"It was buried in the records!" the secretary exclaims. "Covered in dust. I don't think it's ever been read."

"Well read it!" says the prime minister. "Tell me what it says."

The secretary passes the Treaty to the head of government. It's a beautiful Two Row Wampum, the sacred belt of beads that Indigenous and Settler governments used, not long ago, to communicate obligations one to another.

As the prime minister studies the intricate patterns of purple and white, her secretary invites two elders — one Indigenous, the other

Settler—into the office to explain its meaning. With shared understanding, they offer these words:

"In August of 1764, 2,000 chiefs gathered at Niagara to meet with representatives of the British Crown, the ancestors of this Canadian government. The year before, King George III—pressured by Pontiac's war and moved by Quaker Christian cries for justice—issued a Royal Proclamation, which declared that all lands west of the Appalachians were to be 'reserved to the Indians as hunting grounds.' No land could be taken by settler society; not without the consent of the Indigenous.

"The chiefs discussed this new proposal with their communities. With copies of the Proclamation in hand, they prayed and performed ceremony as they discerned its implications. Twenty-four Nations then came together at Niagara to clarify with the Crown the principles that would govern this relationship—principles of peace, mutual respect, and non-interference between sovereign peoples. Your government, prime minister, affirmed these principles, and the Indigenous, in turn, accepted the Proclamation. To ratify the pact, wampum belts—like the one you hold—were exchanged, gifts given, and pipes smoked. The treaty was alive! It was a covenant that was to last forever!"

The prime minister is shocked. She's never heard any of this before. "Why didn't I know this? And why don't we all know the story of this covenant?"

Visibly shaken, she takes off her glasses and starts to weep. Then, very quietly, she talks to herself. Perhaps she's praying. A minute or so later she stands up, straightens her suit, and gives her secretary these orders:

"It's time to redress the wrongs of the past. We haven't honoured our Treaty relationship. No wonder there's no harmony in our land. It's not a native problem. It's our problem. We have betrayed the promises we agreed to. It's a national disgrace. Call my cabinet immediately, and get the governor general here as well. Things are going to change. And soon!"

And the Canadian public marvelled at the prime minister. She did not need to heed the Treaty. She did not need to be alarmed. She did not need to depart from the ways of all other prime ministers. But she did. It would cost her. But she would be remembered because she did right.

Solomon decided to build a temple for the name of the LORD and a royal palace for himself. Solomon conscripted seventy thousand laborers and eighty thousand stonecutters in the hill country, with three thousand six hundred to oversee them.

2 Chronicles 2:1–2

UNMASKING STATE THEOLOGY

Gerald O. West

IN 1 CHRONICLES 17, King David proposes to Nathan the prophet that, since he now lives in "a house of cedar," God too should be located in "a house" rather than "a tent" (verse 1). Initially, Nathan affirms the plan. However, that same night "the word of God came to Nathan" (verse 3), making it clear that God did not approve of David's scheme. God makes it clear to Nathan, who then makes it clear to David, that God dismisses David's proposal on two grounds. First, God's historical choice has been to go "from tent to tent" and from place to place with the people (verses 5–6). Second, the initiative must be God's:

> In all places where I have walked with all Israel, have I spoken a word with any of the judges of Israel, whom I commanded to shepherd My people, saying, "Why have you not built for Me a house of cedar?"(verse 6).

The message to the prophet and to David is unmistakable: God will not be restricted to one place and will not be dictated to by any human leader.

The implied subtext is equally unambiguous for those with an understanding of the power realities of the Ancient Near East. In that context, the people and their territories were controlled religiously, culturally, economically, and politically by two related institutions: the royal court (house) and the temple (house) of God. These two "houses" were the key sites of economic exploitation of the peasant farmers who made up 95 percent of the population. Their lives were controlled by an

82

alliance between these "houses." What David is proposing is the establishment of such an "unholy" alliance. And God makes it clear that God will not be party to such.

So we ought to be suspicious when we come to 2 Chronicles 2 and read that "Solomon decided to build a house for the name of Yahweh and a royal palace for himself" (2:1). God has not asked, yet Solomon has "decided" to build God "a house." Even though Solomon acknowledges that "the heavens and the highest heavens cannot contain God" (verse 6), he persists with his plan to build God "a house." Why? The answer, in today's terms, is what the 1985 South African *Kairos Document* called "State Theology."

> "State Theology" is simply the theological justification of the status quo with its racism, capitalism and totalitarianism. It blesses injustice, canonizes the will of the powerful, and reduces the poor to passivity, obedience and apathy.

Solomon is setting up a system that will legitimate the exploitation of the people. God's "house" will become a crucial component in the establishment of a temple-city state, providing religious justification for an economy of extraction, systematically robbing the peasant farmers of their produce, their livestock, their children, their land, and their very souls. As Samuel the prophet, heeding the word of God (1 Samuel 8:9), had foretold, "The king will take" (verses 11, 13, 14, 15, 16, 17). And how would the king take? By employing a tribute system that was centred in the royal court and the temple. Religion would cloak socio-economic exploitation. City-based elites would become richer and richer and peasant farmers would become poorer and poorer. This economic system would give birth to and nurture the one percent of Ancient Israel.

As we read on in 2 Chronicles 2, exploitation is readily apparent even before the city-temple state economic system is fully established. In order to build the temple, Solomon must borrow from a neighbouring ruler, King Hiram of Tyre (2:3–10). It will become evident later that Solomon has incurred massive debt in the process. How does he repay this debt? He "gives" Israelite cities to Tyre's king:

> It came about at the end of 20 years in which Solomon had built the two houses, the house of the Lord and the king's house… then King Solomon gave Hiram 20 cities in the land of Galilee (1 Kings 9:10–11).

Solomon pays state-incurred debt by selling his people to a neighbouring king. It is little wonder that the Chronicler avoids this part of the narrative, refusing to follow his primary source (1 and 2 Kings) at this point. Rather than condemning Solomon's blasphemous behaviour, the Chronicler chooses to omit this episode. Moreover, in this half-truth re-telling of the Chronicler, we notice how the entire economic transaction between Solomon and the king of Tyre is framed in religious language (2:3–10). Religion is used to cloak exploitation.

The Chronicler is also not fully honest in describing the labour system Solomon uses to build the temple. According to 2 Chronicles 2:17, it is resident "aliens" that form the labour force. But later on, even the Chronicler must confess that Israelites, too, have been used as forced labour. Here the Chronicler does follow his source text (1 and 2 Kings), copying almost exactly the story of 1 Kings 12:1–19 in 2 Chronicles 10:1–19. This is a remarkable narrative, forsaking as it does any theological framing; instead we have a clear account of socio-economic exploitation. When Solomon dies and his son Rehoboam succeeds him, Solomon is not remembered for his "wisdom and knowledge" (2 Chronicles 1:10). He is remembered as a socio-economic tyrant by the majority of his people.

2 Chronicles 10:1–19 uncovers what South Africans today refer to as "state capture." South Africans have become too familiar with this dreadful phrase, as it sums up the range of ways the resources of the state are annexed for the personal enrichment of the elite, robbing the people of resources meant for them. The Israelite state, too, has been captured by the royal house and its associated city-temple based elites. Though the Chronicler tends to omit the negative aspects of the Davidic-Solomonic monarchy as told in 1 and 2 Kings, even the Chronicler must acknowledge "state capture." 2 Chronicles 10:1–19 makes it clear that Solomon has not only extracted excessive tribute from the 10 northern tribes (known as "Israel"), he has also extracted forced labour. Solomon's own people are among the workers who build his temple. Moreover,

Solomon has given preference to his own tribe, the tribe of Judah, by exempting them from his oppressive "yoke" (verse 4). Africans across the continent are familiar with this kind of tribal-patronage in which political leaders favour their "own people" while exploiting those who are not of their tribe.

When Rehoboam succeeds his father Solomon as King, Jeroboam—the leader of the breakaway 10 northern tribes—says to Rehoboam:

> Your father made our yoke hard; now therefore lighten the hard service of your father and his heavy yoke which he put on us, and we will serve you (verse 4).

In what follows, we see the logic of "state capture." Rehoboam is not shocked by his father's oppression. He does not respond immediately with a commitment to "lighten the load." Instead, he consults. Appropriately, he consults with "the elders who had served his father Solomon while he was still alive" (verse 6). They council an alternative economics: "If you will be kind to this people and please them and speak good words to them, then they will be your servants forever" (verse 7). Among these elders, it is likely that there would have been those who remembered a socio-economic system grounded in the communitarian relationships of the pre-monarchic period.

But not hearing what he wants to hear, Rehoboam "forsook the counsel of the elders" and "consulted with the young men who grew up with him and served him" (verse 8). There are two key components to his choice of "the young men." First, Rehoboam consults with those who, like him, are products of the monarchic tributary system and its massive inequalities. They know no other socio-economic system and are direct beneficiaries of it. They are among the one percent. They are wealthy because the majority of their people are poor. Second, these "young men" are under his patronage. They say what they know he wants to hear. And what is this? The "young men" counsel hardline economics and lace their recommendation with sexual bravado:

> Thus you shall say to the people who spoke to you, saying, "Your father made our yoke heavy, but you make it lighter for us." Thus you shall say to them, "My little finger is thicker than my father's loins!

Whereas my father loaded you with a heavy yoke, I will add to your yoke; my father disciplined you with whips, but I will discipline you with scorpions" (verses 10–11).

And what does Rehoboam tell the 10 northern tribes when they convene three days later? The Chronicler's account is matter-of-fact: "The king answered them harshly, and King Rehoboam forsook the counsel of the elders. He spoke to them according to the advice of the young men" (verses 13–14).

For the most part, the Chronicler adopts what the South African *Kairos Document* refers to as a "Church Theology" stance, preferring to re-present economic and political matters in religious terms, much as evangelicals and neo-evangelicals do today. Yet in the face of the clear effects of Solomon's exploitative socio-economic policies, even the Chronicler cannot hide behind "spiritual" rationalizations. In this instance, like the biblical prophets and like the "Prophetic Theology" of the South African *Kairos Document*, the Chronicler speaks truth to power, condemning Rehoboam's perpetuation of Solomon's oppressive socio-economic policies. The narrative concludes by elaborating the death-dealing consequences of Rehoboam's refusal to "listen to the people" (verse 15) and lighten the yoke.

First, the 10 northern tribes rebel, refusing any longer to be a part of an oppressive monarchic system (verse 16). A united Israel will never again exist. Ever. This is the cost of Solomon's systemic socio-economic exploitation. Second, when Rehoboam tries to use force to bring the 10 northern tribes back under his oppressive control, sending "Hadoram, who was over the forced labour," the result is even more violence: "the sons of Israel stoned him to death" (verse 18). Socio-economic oppression leads to rebellion and bloody revolution. Oppressors will be resisted, both in Ancient Israel and in contemporary South Africa. Oppressors will be resisted, even when they veil their oppression in religious language.

Then Ezra the priest stood up and said to them, "You have trespassed and married foreign women, and so increased the guilt of Israel. Now make confession to the LORD the God of your ancestors, and do his will; separate yourselves from the peoples of the land and from the foreign wives."

Ezra 10:10–11

PRAYER OF THE SENT-AWAY

Ryan Dueck

I have a problem with the Bible, but all is not lost. I just need to read it standing on my head. I need to change my perspective. If I can accept that the Bible is trying to lift up those who are unlike me, then perhaps I can read the Bible right.

—Brian Zahnd

DEAR GOD,

Can I call you "dear"? Are you dear to me? Am I dear to you? Sometimes it's hard to say. Sometimes, harder to know.

Anyway, dear God, I have something to say, something to pray on behalf of the sent-away ones, all the women and children who are cast aside, kicked to the curb, blamed and shamed, ignored and forgotten.

This world that you have made is very good at sending people like my children and me away. I think that for as long as human beings have walked this earth, there have been some who thought they were worth more than others. That they were more righteous, more holy, more pure, more clean, more whatever than people with the wrong blood in their veins, the wrong religion, the wrong history, the wrong... well, whatever.

People like me: We don't belong among the righteous, the holy, the pure. We don't fit.

And so we are sent away.

I'm not sure if you know this or not, but a lot of times they use you, dear God, as the reason for sending us away. You've called them, chosen them, set them apart. Or something like that. And they can't be mixed up with women like me. This is what the men of God say, anyway. We're a defective race. We're idolaters. We lead them astray. We are evidence of their sin.

And so we are sent away.

Dear God, we are little people and our voices don't seem to matter much. We don't have a say. We are women and children in a world run by men. We are easy to use and abuse. We always have been. I guess we're a good place to park the blame.

And so we are sent away.

My people aren't very influential. We're a kind of footnote in holy books and history books and all the other books that tell the preferred version of the story. We're a speed bump on the road to holiness or redemption or progress. We've always been disposable.

And so we are sent away.

Dear God, there are all kinds of ways to be sent away, aren't there? We could be banished to the wilderness, like Hagar, or sent packing in the driving rain, like all those poor souls in the days of Ezra.

Or like my people, sent away to boarding schools, isolated from families and communities, lied to by governments, and sequestered in reserves—setting in motion toxic cycles of dysfunction, addiction, loneliness, and violence (and I know you know, dear God, that we women and our children always bear the heaviest costs in these cycles).

We were and we are considered impure. We were and we are a persistent reminder of wrong things done by the right people. We need to be out of sight and out of mind. We are bad for business.

And so we are sent away.

And being sent away, we have discovered, takes a very long time. It effects generations. And it is done over and over and over again. It is done through government policies or casual words on the street. It is done through racist systems and structures or well-intentioned paternalism. It is done through apathy and resignation as much as anything explicitly evil. But the end result is often the same.

We are sent away.

In the name of nation and progress and economy and religion. In the name of God.

But I know better. I know that you do not demand all of this sending away. You can't. You are, after all, one of us. One of the sent-away ones. You know what it is for others to think that you're contaminating their system. You know what it is to be sneered at, ridiculed, misunderstood, mistreated. You know how it feels to be called "dirty," "illegitimate," "sinner," "bastard." You're familiar with messing up the religious rules. You know what it feels like to be sacrificed on the altar of purity.

You know what it is to be sent away, out of sight, out of mind. I guess you, too, were bad for business. But for all of us sent away ones? You're pretty good news. No matter what the holy men say.

And this is why I call you "dear," God. Still.

I said to the king, "May the king live forever! Why should my face not be sad, when the city, the place of my ancestors' graves, lies waste, and its gates have been destroyed by fire?" Then the king said to me, "What do you request?" So I prayed to the God of heaven. Then I said to the king, "If it pleases the king, and if your servant has found favour with you, I ask that you send me to Judah, to the city of my ancestors' graves, so that I may rebuild it."

Nehemiah 2:3–5

THE MOONS OF RENEWAL AND GROWTH

Robert Two Bulls

IT WAS THE MONTH of Magzkscicaagli (Moon When Ducks Come Back) in the second year of Joe "Flying Feather" Jones Jr.'s appointment as the Principal Deputy Assistant Secretary of Indian Affairs for the United States Department of the Interior. At the time I, Wichakigna (One Who Comforts People), was one of his support staff.

After our Monday morning staff meeting, Joe asked, "Why were you quiet? Your face had a look of consternation through most of the meeting."

I replied, "It probably has something to do with the two dreams I had over the weekend and the call I received yesterday from my cousin. In my first dream, I was at a relative's house in one of the housing projects on the Pine Ridge Reservation. Everything seemed gloomy and depressing, and the wind howled outside. There were other folks in the room I didn't recognize, as they all had their heads down as if in prayer. And then suddenly someone started singing the mourning song. That's all I remember.

"The next night I had another vivid dream like the first, but in it, I was standing on a ridge overlooking a wide, mist-covered river valley. Enshrouded in the mist were hundreds of tipis with people walking about. There was laughter and talk. I stood there for what seemed like hours, looking at the beautiful, wonderful sight before my eyes. Suddenly a young child stopped, looked my way and waved. He was beckoning me to come down and join them. As I took a step the dream ended. I woke up happy.

"Then yesterday my cousin called with some sad news about the death of an old friend of ours. He rolled his car somewhere on Mission Flats. He was drinking for two days and was coming back from a beer run when it happened. Now I have been thinking about home, trying to make sense of the dreams and the call."

Then Joe asked, "What are you going to do?"

I quickly said a prayer to God in my heart, and replied, "I'm going to resign from my position and go back home to help rebuild the Oglala Lakota Oyate."

Just then, Mary "Painted Pony Woman" Smith, the Acting Director of the Bureau of Indian Affairs (BIA), came strolling into the office. Joe told her about my dreams, phone call, and resignation.

Mary was surprised. "Why do you want to give up all this to do that?" Waving her arms around, "That's what we do!" she exclaimed. "We provide all the services to better the lives of all American Indians of the Federally Recognized Tribes. You think you can accomplish this?"

"Yes," I replied, "But I need a few favours from you both. I would like it if you can make the necessary contact with all the department and division heads to let them know what my intentions are and what I will need from them. Also, I am hoping that your office can use its leverage to convince the Oglala Sioux Tribal Council to give the go-ahead."

With some hesitation, Mary said, "Well, what the hell, we tried using just about all the ideas that were put on our desk and very little seems to be working."

Joe nodded. "I know, right!? And we have been doing the same thing for decades!"

Mary asked me how long it would take me to accomplish what I was setting out to do. I didn't know, as it was now on God's time and God's hand.

Joe and Mary sent me along the way with letters of permission to begin the work of rebuilding the Oglala Lakota Oyate.

Mary made calls to arrange meetings where I would be asking for certain things to help make this dream a reality. I needed unencumbered access to land, a large herd of buffalo, access to give lectures to school classrooms, lodge poles from the pine forest, and other services for start-up. She contacted the Deputy Bureau Director of Trust Services, the division heads of Natural Resources, Environmental and

Cultural Resources, Land Buy Back, and the Forestry and Wildland Fire Management.

Joe called his Principal Deputy Assistant Secretary to instruct her to contact the Deputy Assistant Secretary of Policy and Economic Development and the Deputy Assistant Secretary of Indian Affairs, to let them know that I would be coming in to see them. These offices in turn called the Deputy Bureau Director of Indian Services and the Division head of Self Determination, as well as the Deputy Bureau Director of Field Operations. The Field Operation guy called the director of the Great Plains Regional Office to let them all know that I would be stopping by to tell them about my dream. Both Mary and Joe sent official letters to the Oglala Sioux Tribal Council and the BIA Superintendent of my intentions.

When I arrived on the reservation and shared my vision to any who would listen, the reaction was both positive and negative. There were those who had similar dreams and also many who joined the ranks of the naysayers. One of them sneered, "That's a fantasy and I don't think anyone really wants to live like our ancestors did in the days of old. It's a pipe dream. Besides, life here is tough and has been this way for years. What makes you think you can actually accomplish this? It will be difficult!"

"It is the time of the moons of renewal and growth," I replied. "God and the Feds are on our side."

And thus we began the work.

Then King Ahasuerus said to Queen Esther and to the Jew Mordecai, "See, I have given Esther the house of Haman, and they have hanged him on the gallows, because he plotted to lay hands on the Jews."

Esther 8:7

THEY WERE ALL CAPTIVE

Sarah Travis

I was Queen Vashti.
Remember me? I was the king's first choice,
until I decided I'd had enough of being an object—
paraded around like a tasty treat before visiting dignitaries.
There was no dignity involved,
so I resisted the king's desires
and I was banished.

I still had eyes and ears inside the palace.

I watched from a distance as
that girl was primped and prepared to replace me.
A Jew.

I knew it, even if his majesty did not;
King Ahasuerus was not as smart as he looked.
Esther certainly was beautiful and witty
(so was I, but she had the benefit of youth).

I both hated and respected her,
an orphan who claimed a voice to speak to the most powerful.
The king offered her half his kingdom and she said no.
She resisted him just like I did,
but did it to protect her own people.
She refused to stay silent when Haman declared war on the Jews—

she risked her own life to negotiate with the king
(he was not as potent as he liked to believe).

It's amazing, really, what she and Mordecai accomplished.
Haman hung on his own gallows.
I'm not sure he deserved it—
wasn't he just caught in the king's web too?
Esther and Mordecai were given carte blanche
to rewrite the law of the land—
a decree sealed with the King's ring
so that the Jews could fight back against their attackers.

A great reversal of fortune.
It would not be the Jews who died,
but the whole House of Haman—
some guilty, some innocent.
Is that justice? Is anyone safe
when the master's own tools
are used to dismantle the master's house?
Mordecai wore that gold crown and those royal robes
very proudly when he left the palace.
How quickly he abandoned his oppression
and learned to walk like a prince.

The Jews celebrated in the streets,
but I'm not sure what they were celebrating.
Nobody won that day.
They were all captive to a system beyond their control,
yet none of them could see it—
not Haman and his family, not the Jews,
not the king's secretaries,
not Mordecai, not Esther,
not the king himself.

Maybe history will learn its lesson.
Maybe, women like Esther, women like me,
will resist the systems that try to keep us

silent and vulnerable.
Maybe women and men will use the opportunities they have to bring life, not death.

You too were born for such a time as this.

The LORD said to Satan, "Have you considered my servant Job? There is no one like him on the earth, a blameless and upright man who fears God and turns away from evil." Then Satan answered the LORD, "Does Job fear God for nothing?"

Job 1:8–9

THE TRUTH OF *BIMAADIZIWIN*

Kathy Moorhead Thiessen

THERE ONCE WAS a very good man who lived in the land of Manitowapow (the narrows of the Great Spirit). When he was born, his mother looked at his tiny face and said, "He is a job well done!" and the name Job stayed with him. Every part of his life reflected the truth of *Mino Bimaadiziwin* (the Good Life). He treated all people and the creation around him with love, respect, courage, honesty, wisdom, humility, and truth.

Job and his wife had seven sons and three daughters. They taught the children the skills they needed to live well, and the family and all those in the community benefitted from the bounty of their hunting, fishing, trapping and gathering. Many came to Job for advice and acted on his wisdom.

His children would often gather friends for times of celebration. Afterwards, Job took time to speak with each of them. He wanted to find out if they had acted in good ways in their gatherings. He guided each of them to use the smudge and prayer to connect with Creator.

One day, Creator was watching the goings-on in the big city of Muddy Waters, where the Red and Assiniboine Rivers meet. Creator saw men in business suits enter a high-rise office. Big Boss, sitting behind a big oak desk, asked what they were up to. They said that they were going here and there, in the woods and through the rivers, seeking to discover where the untapped resources lay. They spoke of the things they wanted to get their hands on: the wood in the forests, the gold in the rock, the oil lying below the surface, and the power of the waters. They spoke fervently about the money that could flow into the region and into their pockets. And they complained about the resistance that they faced from "those Indians."

Big Boss said, "I know of this Anishinaabe man, Job, who lives up North. We have had many good conversations, and he listens to reason. He could be persuaded to talk to the people to get them to step down."

The men in suits agreed, "We have heard of this man. Maybe you are right, but it may take a little more force to get him to speak the way we want him to."

Big Boss cautioned, "Do what you need to do, but don't hurt him. There will be very bad press if word gets out."

The men went out and put on their leisure clothes, smiling faces, and smooth-talking voices. They journeyed to Job's territory and spent many hours with him describing their plans. "There will be many jobs and much money for your people." "We will immediately plant many trees to replace the ones we take." "This will be good for the ecosystem, just like the natural process of a forest fire." "The animals will come to your land to eat the plants that will grow." "Your people will benefit from the riches of the gold we will find." "Many of your people drive trucks; they need the oil too." And on and on.

Job listened carefully. After all the words, he decided to trust these men. And he decided that the industry could help his people.

Immediately, and over the next months and years, the big trucks, tree harvesters, diggers, and drillers came to extract the trees, the gold, and the oil.

One day as Job was eating breakfast, he heard an urgent knock on his door. A man from the community told him that he had discovered, deep in the forest, that men in huge machines had cleared all the trees. They had dug up the medicines and destroyed the trap lines. While he was speaking, another community member came rushing in. He expressed dismay at how the use of oil and the chopping of trees had changed the days of rain and sun. Drought had made the forest like dry tinder and one lightning bolt had started a huge fire. It burned acres of the remaining forest, including the hunting grounds that had fed the community. He told of two families who had not escaped from their cabins and had been burned alive.

Soon, an old woman came as quickly as she could. She spoke of poverty and hunger because the animals that had previously been harvested for food had run away. They had no cover in the forest due to the clear-cut and fires. Job offered her some bannock and meat stew. They sat down together to hear more of her story.

As they were talking, a young woman came running up, gasping for breath. Through her tears she told Job that she had been at a party with many of the children of the community, including his sons and daughters. The wealth that had come with the new industry gave resources to buy much alcohol and drugs. Many of the young people had been overcome with intoxication, and some of them had died.

Job cried out in anguish.
He cut off his long braid to show his grief.

Job's decision to find good things for his people had relied on the integrity of the men in suits. Their deception had brought poverty, hunger, and death. Creator looked upon Job with compassion. Creator told Job to continue to live in the truth of *Mino Bimaadiziwin*—love, respect, courage, honesty, wisdom, humility, and truth.

How long, O LORD? Will you forget me forever? How long must I bear pain in my soul, and have sorrow in my heart all day long? How long shall my enemy be exalted over me?

Psalm 13:1−2

WILL YOU WALK?

Leah Gazan

Am I invisible to you?

Objectified by the colonizer,
who has taken my beautiful brown body
to be abused,
to be used,
to be exploited
by corporate corruption
that perpetrates violence against me
and our Mother Earth that feeds all life.

Do you understand who I am?

Outside of colonial stereotypes
that have defined me as
a mystical Indian Princess,
a sexy squaw whose body
is there for the taking
like Pocahontas,
a little girl who became a commodity,
John Smith's prize,
a celebrated story of violation.

Do you see me?
I see you.

Your cold shoulder is a clear answer
defined by your privilege to turn a blind eye
to the walls that have been carefully constructed
through legislation to imprison me,
leaving me vulnerable to violence
that attempts to beat down my spirit
and silence my voice.

Do you understand I will not be broken?

I will keep walking forward
to the beat of 1,000 years of resiliency
gifted to me by my ancestors,
guiding me to keep fighting,
to keep fighting,
to keep fighting,
to keep fighting
for the light that shines
from the wisdom bestowed on me
by my grandmothers
whose warrior cries keep me awake
and free.

Do you recognize the power of one's heart?

It is a guiding force,
my weapon of strength and kindness
to protect our beautiful Mother Earth,
whose DNA flows through my blood memory,
inspiring courage not to be frightened
by the weak acts of misogynistic aggression
that pale in comparison to the strong
heartbeat of our Mother.

Do you hear me?

I share my story with you

to help you understand
I am a mother,
I am a daughter,
I am a sister,
I am an auntie,
whose heart has the power to fight
for a new day where Indigenous bodies
are honoured.

Our ancestors need to rest
knowing our spirits are free
from the shameless violence
rooted in a foundation of hate
by those who have tried to oppress us.

Will you walk with me?

I am waiting for you
to go on an adventure
on the road of gentleness, kindness, and love
towards a new tomorrow,
carrying the strength
of thousands of years of hope
much stronger than the weak colonial structures
that are easily broken by the heart of a woman
whose body has the power
to maintain the Circle of Life.

May he defend the cause of the poor of the people, give deliverance to the needy, and crush the oppressor.

Psalm 72:4

SEE THE COLONIZING MANDATE

Stan McKay

WE ARE LIVING today amidst incredible violence and rumours of nuclear war. A form of democracy is being promoted that is anything but the peoples' rule; it is shaped by privilege and twisted by corporate power. The wealth of the northern regions is protected through military might and hegemonic legal structures, while the Two-Thirds world is gripped by devastating poverty and is victimized by the established systems. A reading of Psalm 72 is prescient as we search for ways to imagine good governance for nation-states in our current global context.

The Psalm is attributed to Israel's infamous King Solomon. It is a prayer to address the injustices of the world. It is a prayer that the king and his son be gifted by God so that they may be righteous judges who defend the poor and conquer the oppressor. Psalm 72 is clear. God's king will have pity on the needy and will function as a redeemer. The people will be blessed by this king.

But a closer reading of the Psalm and its author raises serious questions. Solomon, the child of an unfaithful relationship, may have gifts of wisdom and vision, but he is utterly adulterous in his relationships with women, money, the people, and the land. Solomon acquires 700 wives who are pawns in his accumulation of influence with other nations. Solomon builds an opulent temple for God, but builds a house for himself that is even bigger and better. Solomon builds up a standing army with chariots and horses, and conscripts the masses into forced labour. Solomon is the epitome of abusive power and privilege.

In Psalm 72, we read the prayer for an everlasting universal kingdom that will be built in peace and sustained in peace. How? By keeping the inhabitants in submission. The Holy One of Israel will raise his people out of the depths — and secure his title — through hereditary royalty and the divine right of kings.

And what is the result of this divine rule? The prayer lifts up nature and harvest imagery, comparing justice and righteousness under the king to abundant crops, fruit orchards, blossoming grass, and the shining of the sun. The references remind me of later covenants and treaties on Turtle Island, in which Indigenous nations were invited to support the British monarch, who would, in turn, bring both bounty and power while maintaining dominion over the earth.

When the Treaty Commissioners, acting on behalf of the Crown, did their work across western Canada in the 1870s, they made repeated references to the Queen and her benevolence. They described her as "our Great White Mother." They assured Indigenous peoples that she was righteous and that she would care for them. In turn, Indigenous peoples agreed to share life on this land with the Settlers and to live together in peace.

And yet the result has been anything but peace for Indigenous peoples. We have been marginalized and abused by an imperial process described as colonization. Many of the principles that guided the Crown and her Settlers can be found in the verses of Psalm 72. Power, privilege, and a divine sense of mandate did not liberate the oppressed, but oppressed the needy. Indeed, Solomon's vision for the "good life" led Canada and Canadian churches to create Indian Residential Schools and fund missions that fractured our communities, took us from the land, and promoted cultural genocide. And sadly, frustratingly, the same power and privilege is at work today. We need a different psalm, a new prayer, and a real covenant.

By the rivers of Babylon—
there we sat down and there we
wept when we remembered Zion.

Psalm 137:1

RECONCILED

Rarihokwats

By the shores of the Athabasca, there we sit down,
and there we weep when we remember the way it was
when Creator gave it to sustain our lives.

There we gave gratitude for our gifts,
the pure water we could drink from a cup,
the abundance of fish to sustain the lives of our children,
now only memories of who we were.

They ask us to be grateful for "progress,"
for "development," for the "civilization" they have given us.
Now they ask us to dance in their parades,
to put on our feathers for their amusement,
while our children learn of Champlain, Cartier, Cabot
and are told, "Beat that drum and do your chants!"

We are on the same shores,
but it is no longer the same river.
How can we say, "Thank you, Creator?"

I will never forget you, Athabasca, as you were meant to be.
I will teach my children of the way you were
here in our Promised Land. We will restore you to health.

What good am I if I do not remember who you are?

Psalm 137

If I do not remember who I am,
not what I have become,
if I do not make what you were
a vision for my children?

I remember all those who took my language,
who took my culture, who took me from my parents and people.

"Kill the Indian in the child!" "Kill the Indian!"
And now I am all that is left.

My mind wants retribution, repayment, restitution,
for what you have done to us.
I struggle with thoughts of hate.
Of violence. Even violence against my own self.

But what little remains of my culture tells me
those were not Creator's instructions for me
when I was given life.
We must restore our lives, our values,
our Elder's teachings.
We must embrace and
see what lives we might make for our children
who have a right to their own Promised Land
on the shores of our Athabasca
restored to health.

He declares his word to Jacob,
his statutes and ordinances to
Israel. He has not dealt thus with
any other nation; they do not know
his ordinances. Praise the LORD!

Psalm 147:19–20

YOU ALONE LISTENED

Lori Ransom

Greetings and thanks be to you,
Creator, Spirit, Holy Mystery.

How good it is at each day's end
to sit before the sacred fire,
to place tobacco in the flames, and
to pour out my heart to you, with my tears.

I have spent
another day gathering statements
for the Truth and Reconciliation Commission of Canada,
listening to the heart-shaped stories
of survivors and others who have experienced residential schools,
or the legacy of the schools.

What a profound privilege it is to spend time
with those who have chosen to make their statements
to the Commission *in private.*
As one of the very few to hear their stories,
I give thanks to you for this sacred trust.
I am grateful for the family members and friends
who accompany those giving statements.
I am grateful for the small, comfortable room
in which we do our work.
I am grateful for the presence of our sacred medicines:

cedar, sage, sweetgrass, tobacco.
I am grateful for the support of the videographer
and the health support worker.

We do this difficult work alone,
away from the bright lights and big crowds
in the Public Statement Gathering and Sharing Circle rooms.
I send my praise and thanksgiving to you, Creator,
for being present in all of these places and for listening with us.

You alone listened each and every day, year in and year out,
to these same adults when they were children
attending residential schools, and to the generations
of children who attended these schools before them —
those who never had a chance to make statements
to anyone other than you.

You alone listened to their parents,
and to the other adults left behind
in First Nations, Métis, and Inuit communities,
bereft of the presence of their little ones.
What is a community without children?
You alone listened to members of families
as they struggled to cope with isolation from one another,
broken apart by outside forces.

Today, you listen to the children
and grandchildren of survivors
about what it was like to be raised
by adults who were parented
by cold and uncaring institutions.

You alone know the names
of our missing children
who never came home,
names given to them in the languages
into which they were born.

You alone know where they rest,
and it is you who gives them peace.
They shine in your Light eternally
like the stars in the sky.

You alone will judge the oppressors,
those who created and sustained
the destructive system of colonizing education,
those who violated our babies in the darkness.

With resilience, and to the beat of our drums,
we give you praise and greetings,
as in the Thanksgiving Address
of my Haudenosaunee relatives.

We give our thanks and greetings,
        to the winds and the snow,
        to the sunshine and the clouds,
        to the vegetation that feeds us.

We give our thanks and greetings
        to the lands which sustain us and our relatives in Creation,
        to the four-legged creatures,
        to the winged ones in the skies, and
        to the beings that swim
        in the rivers and lakes and oceans.

We give our thanks and praise,
        for all the tears shed at this
        Truth and Reconciliation Commission event
        as you grieve with us,
        and for the peace you give us,
        which passes all understanding.

Creator, you restore us.
You sustain our communities
and strengthen our people's spirits of resilience

as we rebuild.
You are the Great Healer of our broken minds,
our broken spirits, our broken hearts.
You cleanse our abused bodies as no human can.

Creator, you challenge me to be a warrior
in support of those in my community
whose hurts run too deep for telling,
those who find it difficult to be heard,
those who are forgotten,
those who are misunderstood
or subject to racism and hatred.

You have spoken to the Indigenous peoples of the lands
—now called Canada—from time immemorial.
You have shared unique wisdom and knowledge
with every nation of the First Peoples.
You entrusted this sacred knowledge
to the care of our Elders, teachers, and storytellers.

I pray that I will use what I have learned from them well,
that I will honour all my relations in the created world,
in everything I say and do
from the time I wake up in the morning
to the time I put my body to rest at night.

You alone listen to me and my colleagues,
who gathered the thousands of survivors' stories,
each of us entrusted to help
carry memory-burdens of past suffering
for the sake of helping others to heal,
to reconcile with loved ones,
and even to reconcile with you.

We give you thanks for renewing our strength
each day to continue the journey to which you have called us.
Thanks be to God!

Do not rob the poor because they are poor, or crush the afflicted at the gate; for the LORD pleads their cause and despoils of life those who despoil them.

Proverbs 22:22–23

TODAY, KNOW THIS

Robert O. Smith

PROVERBS OF THE ELDERS. Received wisdom. The common sense of the ages. Men speaking to men, warning of loose women. Disjointed aphorisms, speaking against the Other, made known to us today.

Today, the Proverbs tell us, "Do not remove the ancient landmark that your ancestors have set up." But we must ask: Who are our ancestors? Which landmarks are ancient? What is worth remembering?

In our land, history has been crafted from contempt, our ancestors enslaved and sold, our ancestors forced to march to new lands.

Our ancestors were despoiled of land, the very source of life. The common sense of the ages tells us: they are the ones at fault.

Our ancestors were made to serve those who became our gleaming white kings. In our land, slavery was more than a metaphor.

Today's tin-pot kings erect and protect tinfoil monuments to Cornwallis and Lee. They tell us who our ancestors truly are. Generals represent the general sense.

Today is the time for new proverbs, new wisdom to fill our hearts.

The false monuments will be torn down, crumpled like wasted paper. The knowledge we carry in our bones will persist.

The monuments of our ancestors are set up in our breasts. We carry them along the way: retelling their stories, refreshing their memories, singing their songs anew, nourishing our children so they will not stray.

Our children will hear the stories of our peoples — Slave, Indigenous, and Settler. They will hear how the Lord keeps watch over knowledge and overthrows the words of the faithless.

Those who protect injustice, inequality, and inhumanity will suffer calamity; their reign of terror will cease. States and stock markets will end; the land and its peoples will endure.

We will not hide how gender, greed, race, and religion justified genocide and theft. We will place new plaques in the parks so all can know the former kings' feet of clay.

We will replace the shaken foundations; new sovereignties will be made. We will give true answers to those who have brought us forth.

Incline your ear and apply your mind to this teaching. It is not pleasant. The past and the present bring pain. Our anger will never be suppressed for the sake of comfort.

We will seek truth. We will seek justice. With these in hand, we will seek reconciliation. In pure heart and direct speech, we challenge the Settler to be a friend.

I am black and beautiful,
O daughters of Jerusalem, like the
tents of Kedar, like the curtains of
Solomon.

Song of Songs 1:5

NO FENCE CAN HOLD

Cheryl Bear

how do i let him know
i want to feel his lips on mine
i want him to kiss me deep
for this love is calming
exhilarating
addicting
he always smells like outside
like a forest freshly washed with rain
my heart flares when
someone says his name
i blush
surprised at that reaction, i blush more
a reaction common to women, i've noticed
and they have every reason
for he is a mountain lion

but
i am dark
brown skin does not reflect
a dark soul
but it does for me

the warm sun soaks into my skin
yet a cold moon wrenched my heart
with secrets darker than my flesh

this i cannot reveal
i cover my face, hiding from every eye, every whisper
i wish he could take me far from this place
the cave of condemnation that is my mind
my family doesn't get it
i'm buried and burned by their words
so much that
i forget to care for myself

i said to him
this one who is always on my mind
where are you
how do i find you
i long to know everything about you

he said, oh lovely one
follow my deep, ancient footprints
you will find me
you will track me until i catch you
i will always stand up for you
you remind me of a spirited young appaloosa
no fence can hold you
you're blinding, dazzling
like trying to look at a river
flashing with sunlight

my friends brought me medicine from soil
scraped from the claws of a great bear
taken from the heart of the mountains
to make me strong and brave
but nothing is better than the scent of this man
he brings that outside fragrance inside
he holds himself strong to a most vulnerable place
like running on ice in spring
making the dam break wide open
he is so tender we are safe from everything
in each other's arms

our love is a cedar longhouse made only for us
i trust this man more than i trust anyone
there is no shame, no fear, only
deep and effortless love

Surely he has borne our
infirmities and carried our
diseases; yet we accounted
him stricken, struck down by
God, and afflicted. But he was
wounded for our transgressions,
crushed for our iniquities;
upon him was the punishment
that made us whole, and by his
bruises we are healed.

Isaiah 53:4—5

A TRUE RECKONING

Darrin W. Snyder Belousek

WE CAN'T BELIEVE IT! The word is that he was God's servant, God's righteous one. And that we're supposed to listen to him and obey his teaching. *Him?!*

What good did God ever do by him? He was nothing from the day he was born. Who was his father? No one knows for sure. Where was he from? A nowhere town that produced nobody good. Who were his teachers? He never even went to school. What did he accomplish? Nothing worth remembering. No one admired him. He had a reputation for associating with undesirables — poor peasants, diseased outcasts. The wealthy and educated classes despised him, the political and religious leaders rejected him. And then came the day he died. Anyone who ends up like that must have been cursed. If he were the blessed one, God would have spared him an ugly death. Apparently, God too despised and rejected him.

That's what we thought. But now I must confess: We were mistaken. About him. And about God.

The truth is this: He bore the burden of all that was wrong in us. All the sickness, suffering, and sorrow of our people, he took upon himself. He took on what was wrong and made putting things right his cause — and he suffered the worst for it. It looked to us like he had been afflicted with a curse. We reckoned that *he* was the unrighteous one, a rebel against God's law — and that *God* had struck him down with disease and death because of his own sin. But we reckoned wrong. No, he was struck down because of *our* sin. Our rebellion inflicted his wounds; our sins destroyed his life. God didn't strike him down. *We* did.

He did not deserve death, but we did. And yet, the pain and punishment that we imposed on him worked out for our peace. God was working in all this. God did not strike him down. Nor did God strike us down for striking him down. Instead, God was putting us right, we who had done him wrong. Though we wounded him, God healed us through his wounds. Though we crushed him, God made us whole through him. We turned from God and went our way, but God chose him to bear our burden so that he might turn us back to God.

Now we see his death for what it truly was — a perversion of justice. He was righteous before God; he never destroyed the innocent, deceived the widow, defrauded the poor, bribed a judge, or blasphemed God. But we tried him on fabricated charges, convicted him by false witnesses, and sentenced him to die. Despite this injustice, he said nothing in his defence. When we mistreated him, he did not vow vengeance against us. His silence testified to our guilt and his trust in God's justice.

He died for us, the righteous one for the unrighteous many — that's the truth. We judged him a transgressor against God, but he interceded with God, petitioning forgiveness for us. He gave up his life as an offering to God for our forgiveness; he died repairing the breach caused by our injustice. For this, God rewarded him: God vindicated him — and forgave us. We have been made righteous again.

God's servant has prospered! God's justice is accomplished!

¤

I can't believe it! Someone is calling *him* a prophet, a martyr, saying we should listen to his message and learn from his example. *Him?!*

I heard talk about him while growing up in our small Midwestern town. Hardly a good word, though. When his name was mentioned, it was mocked: "Maaahtin." He did no good for his own people, much less the whole country, people said. He stirred up problems, broke the law, disturbed the peace. He was a minister of the church, but he strayed from his calling and preached a "social gospel" that distorted the truth. He campaigned for "equality," which is a fine idea, but his "dream" for America seemed utopian and his talk of "justice" for the poor sounded too much like communism. He was a "nigger" who forgot his place and paid the price. To some, the only good thing to be said about him was that he was dead.

He was murdered, but he got what he deserved. He ratcheted up racial tension with his fiery rhetoric. He preached love but provoked a backlash of hate by his confrontational tactics. He divided the country, setting black against white, minority against majority. He defied the authorities that God ordained by his marches and sit-ins, replacing the rule of law with the rule of the mob. He forced the issue into the face of others—and they forced it back at him. In the end, the chain of cause-and-effect that he set in motion came around to kill him.

That's what we thought. But now, I must confess: We were mistaken. About him. And about God.

The truth is this: He bore the burden of what is wrong in us. The evils of racism, materialism, and militarism that corrupt our country, he took upon himself. He took on what was wrong and made putting things right his cause—and he suffered the worst for it. We reckoned that *he* was the unrighteous one, he was the one straying from God's way and defying God's authority—and his end proved us right. But we reckoned wrong. In truth, *our* hatred destroyed him, our violence struck him down, our racism justified his murder. One bullet pierced him, one finger pulled the trigger, one eye sighted the gun. But behind the deeds of one were the desires of many: *We* killed him.

He did not deserve death, but our racism, hatred, and violence did. Yet, despite our evildoing against him, God brought good from his life—for our good. His message of dignity and equality has spread throughout the world; his example of nonviolence has been replicated in other movements; his vision of the Beloved Community has been passed down to future generations.

I now see his death for what it truly was—a perversion of justice. We judged him for breaking the law, but our law was unjust. We accused him of breaching the peace, but our peace enforced oppression. Despite repeated threats against his life, he threatened only to love his enemies in return.

He died for our freedom—that's the truth. He gave up his life so that chains of racism and oppression might be broken, so that one day all people might live together in justice and harmony. Because of him, now I too can sing the song and join the movement: "We're marching on to freedom land..."

God's servant is vindicated! God will bring justice to victory!

The spirit of the Lord GOD is upon me, because the LORD has anointed me; he has sent me to bring good news to the oppressed, to bind up the brokenhearted, to proclaim liberty to the captives, and release to the prisoners.

Isaiah 61:1

THE JEWISH INDIGENOUS *AFTER*

Marc H. Ellis

AS A JEW of Conscience in solidarity with the Palestinian people, I've seen it all, spoken the truth for 30 years and counting. Has it really been that long? The results are meagre. Plying the circuit, I've been raised up and beaten down, lauded and threatened with a Holocaust-like death—by Jews. Rarely have I met Jew or non-Jew neutral on the subject of Israel's oppression of Palestinians.

The *I* is collective. All Jews of Conscience feel the sting. We channel Isaiah and, through Isaiah, God. Still, we're being blown out on the justice trail.

According to Isaiah, Jews have been anointed—or at least commanded—to be a light unto the nations. From God. In biblical language this means justice and reconciliation. So pray tell, Isaiah, what do I and we Jews of Conscience say to Palestinians in Gaza, in the West Bank, in Jerusalem, without becoming bearers of false hope?

As Isaiah knew well, false hope is the most serious breach. Our testimony must be truthful. Is it? Are Palestinians to be rescued by us? Their plight is much worse and longer—50 years, 70 years, and counting—with no end in sight. As Jews of Conscience, we should announce freedom to Palestinian captives. We should offer Palestinians bouquets of roses rather than ashes. If justice still doesn't happen, though, our vision is fraudulent.

Yes, Jews of Conscience hear God's call through Isaiah. We witness the rubble of bombed-out buildings in Gaza, flattened by Israel's Star of David Helicopter Gunships, still in ruins years later; shall Jews of Conscience continue to trumpet Isaiah's call as if the time of blessing will soon arrive? God of liberation, when? Plowshares, Isaiah, how?

131

If God's time is no time, for those in the ruins, waiting is real time. God, answer us! Isaiah, respond! When shall the captive Gazans go free?

Our dilemma is clear. Isaiah's call, God's command, has to be bracketed. Kept in the background. Moved to the back burner, lest we render false testimony and enter that most forbidden realm of idolatry.

Our dilemma deepens, since Isaiah's call and God's demand are canonical, righteous, right on the mark, and in continuity with the rest of the Bible. Yet they aren't happening. Not even close. Indeed, the hope of new life is absent in Palestine. By reading Isaiah's words, do we breathe hope into despair or deflect the truth, that no one, not even God, is interested in rescuing Palestine?

As in the Holocaust, then, we are thrown back on God's unfulfilled promises and, to be honest, God's absence. So that Jews of Conscience, who embody the Jewish Indigenous, do so without God? But then, what can Jews of Conscience proclaim to the Palestinians? Without giving false hope? Without crossing the red line of idolatry?

Isaiah in our time.
With an empowered Israel.
After the Holocaust.

Jewish life now being *after* the Holocaust. And *after* Israel, meaning after what Jews have done and are doing to the Palestinian people. The *afters* being without God.

Jews of Conscience are fighting with words and in the street to deal with these afters. Unsuccessfully.

Hope fades. A rational take on things says that the situation for Palestinians can only get worse. This prediction seems counter-intuitive. The facts on the ground are bad enough.

Jews of Conscience keep banging our ethical heads against an imperial wall. Will we have to exit the community that should be hearing Isaiah's call but isn't? But won't?

Exile it is, once again. The place where Isaiah and so many prophets find their voice. Yet strangely, Isaiah foresaw the fortunes of Israel restored. And indeed, they have been. In our time. Disastrously so.

Today, Jews of Conscience write and act the end of ethical Jewish history, like Isaiah and the prophets who came before. And after.

O LORD, you have enticed me, and I was enticed; you have overpowered me, and you have prevailed. I have become a laughingstock all day long; everyone mocks me. For whenever I speak, I must cry out, I must shout, "Violence and destruction!" For the word of the LORD has become for me a reproach and derision all day long.

Jeremiah 20:7 – 8

LAMENT ON COAST SALISH LAND

Benjamin Hertwig and Céline Chuang

I

O unending Creator, centre of the circle,
in whom all things live, move, and have their being,
how long will the unjust flourish, the pipelines snake over sacred water?
How long before missing women find home and children return to
    arms of kin,
before the Downtown Eastside flows with bannock and blessing?
How long, O Lord?

Céline:

In the Downtown Eastside, where I work, 75 percent of those
who come to the women's centre are Indigenous. Many are not
from here—the territory of the Musqueam, Squamish, and Tsleil-
Waututh—but from across Turtle Island: Cree, Métis, Dene, Gitxsan,
Blackfoot, Wet'suwet'en, Anishinaabe. When land is taken away, trauma
begets trauma, displacement and poverty compound with time. Here,
in the Downtown Eastside, living palimpsest and epicentre of struggle,
the Women's Memorial March was born. A small group of Indigenous
women, eyes wet with weeping, proclaim their grief in public, refuse
state-sanctioned silence.

Whenever I speak, I cry out.

134

This year, my first as a guardian, I wear a reflective vest and walk along-side the Elders' van. The women are old now, 27 years after the first march, slow-moving, frail in body and bone, but still burning with fire. At each stop they lay roses and honour the murdered and missing with ceremony. From their circle, smoke rises to the sky. Thousands follow the Elders past crumbling facades and condemned single room occupancies, luxury boutiques, high-end furniture stores. Three eagles spiral overhead. The drums sound.

Surely now, as we proclaim the women still being stolen — by the housing and fentanyl crises, by men, by prisons and police, by silence — you will turn your face towards those who grieve in public, who cry over sullied land and water, over every street corner.

I am weary of holding it in; indeed, I cannot.

II

God of hosts, are you not Creator of all that is good?
Do you not dwell here too, on Coast Salish territory,
where we so often acknowledge the land
with words alone
yet meet Indigenous death with silence?
Where families are born on the frontline,
births bruised by colonial blow,
where we say "unceded" but not "occupied"
for that would make us the occupiers:
How do we partake in our portion of rage?

Benjamin:
Tina Fontaine and Colten Boushie did not die on Coast Salish territory, where I currently live, but the grief of their death extends from prairie to ocean and back.

Unto you a child is born.

135

Creator called into the world a song so beautiful that the ocean roars with salt and joy. But the music is broken by those claiming to carry it. The music is plucked from the air and fished from the water, hammered into a blade, the trees cut down and burned. Birth becomes death. It was not always this way, and the children wish it had not been so. Two not-guilty verdicts, 13 days apart, two dead. These deaths join many.

The mothers have brought their young to the protest, the organizers' righteous fatigue and fury flow from the first memorial unto the next. The smell of burning sweetgrass in the shadow of the CBC building, drums awake with anger and memory.

Wailing in the morning, a battle cry at noon.

One of the signs reads "Canada is a serial killer of Indigenous people." Those who stand in front of the gathered crowd—some Settler, many Indigenous—are tired. They say as much. Tired of marching and gathering, tired of trying to get the people to listen, tired of Settlers turning their gaze elsewhere, tired of Canada trampling what was and remains good. They gather for future generations, for the children and water and trees. For the creatures that swim, fly, walk. They gather with and without hope.

This is the way of all prophets. They speak in languages that the powerful do not want to hear, sing songs that unsettle, take up space that Canada has taken away. They praise the Creator and lament the brokenness. They stand on the land and mourn. They walk with the land and pray. The music is taken back, the blades bent and stretched into drums, into protest, into forms once forbidden.

III

Does your subaltern Spirit hover now over holy waters,
waves restless with plastic, teeming with creation's hungry ghosts?
Hoarse-throated and aching, our voices join the land defenders.
Children of diaspora, we join the march with unbound feet,
follow the drum beats and pillar of fire,
prepare food and songs for the exodus from empire.

Céline:

My grandmother, who lives in Hong Kong, prays with eyes clenched in a stream of Hokkien syllables, married my grandfather in a white wedding dress, a Western wedding. My grandfather once told me in his best English: do not lose your culture. But how much was already lost before I had hands to carry? How do I carry the weight of colonial Canadian history as a diasporic Christian Settler who has lost the names of my own ancestors? And so I form patterns of kinship. I sing the Women's Warrior Song beside Elders and matriarchs, accept this and other gifts: smoked salmon from a Gitxsan friend, who prays over me with a rumbly voice, moccasins from a Métis mother bonded to me through Benjamin's prairie past.

I am learning that Indigenous joy is a fire that draws others around its circle. I am learning that joy erupts as protest and survival, like it does in Jeremiah, like it does in gospel and jazz and powwow. That praise makes your body move. That exaltation is part of lament, is part of a grief that must keep grieving, breathing, sweating, resisting, creating, demanding.

IV

O God, O God, have you forsaken us?
Across your planet, floodwaters rise.
We tremble instead of heeding your voice,
watch your children cry out
without changing our ways.
When will the scales fall from our eyes?
When, Creator, will we see the world restored?
How deep our thorn, our curse, our cut:
How long, O Lord?

Benjamin:

When I move to the coast from Treaty 6 territory, I live in a room in a house I find on Craigslist. The basement is moldy and the house has rats, but I have a place to stay, somewhere safe to sleep and a view of trees over the street.

In fall, when the leaves are turning and the horse chestnuts have fallen, someone screams from the alley. My housemates and I run over from the porch.

The life of the needy, the hands of the wicked.

An Indigenous woman is on the ground, gathering what is left of her possessions, gathering what is left when so much has already been taken away. The attacker is far away, his shape blending in with the dark. She speaks to us briefly then walks down the alley, alone.

Where are you, good Creator, when women are attacked in alleys? When the trans and two-spirited are born into bodies already targeted? When land is stolen and treaties broken? When the families of Colten Boushie and Tina Fontaine weep? Where are you when the children are taken away?

Then my cousin Hanamel came to me in the court of the guard, in accordance with the word of the LORD, and said to me, "Buy my field that is at Anathoth in the land of Benjamin, for the right of possession and redemption is yours; buy it for yourself." Then I knew that this was the word of the LORD.

Jeremiah 32:8

REMEMBER THAT SPOT?

Peter Haresnape

Remember that spot on the river, past the fork?

Eh?

You know, the spot by the bank just below the fork. East side. We went fishing there in—

—Oh yeah. There. Yeah.

So that spot—

—That was good fishing. Nice shade, and quiet. Did we catch anything?

Sure! I pulled in a—

—Don't tell me, all your fish stories are the same... Just kidding!

Hah! No respect for my skills as a fisherman-storyteller.

Don't get sore.

Eh.

Heh.

So I was down there the other day. Do you know what your uncle Carl saw?

I guess he didn't tell me about it.

Your uncle Carl saw a canoe—

—Uh huh—

—*But not on the water—*

—Uh huh—

—*Under the water. Drifting along under the water, with the current, bumping off the rocks. Spooky, like a ghost canoe. Like a fish, gliding, he said.*

Huh. What was wrong with it? Sprung a leak?

It was just under the water.

Did he get it?

Eh?

Did he fish it out?

Nooo. Too cautious, that one.

Ha. Reminds me of my dad. He took me down there one time but, didn't wanna hop the fence. Thought there was someone watching. Cops, private security, or some shit. We got back in and drove home.

Huh. Your grandmother and her friends used to squeeze under that fence, beside the road.

Where by the road?

Where it crosses the creek bed. The fence was crooked, you could slip under it—

I did it too. So did your dad. Those girls, they used to spend all day there. All night. Stargazing, gossiping. They watched a meteor shower for three nights. Years later we heard about it on the CBC, all these people driving out from the city to see it. They had it in their calendars. And those girls were just there because that's where they went. All summer long.

All summer.

No school, so back to the river. Try to forget some of that English. But not too much.

That fence is pretty solid now. And they hate when we go over.

No "forgive us our trespassing"?

Uh, I guess not? Janine and Psych got a ticket from the cops. They took it to court, you know? Next thing you know they're messaging me, asking for fuckin' genealogies and treaties and charters. Trying to show their "inherent and Treaty Aboriginal rights." Bullshit. Would have cost them thousands. So they paid the ticket.

Those cops don't want people going in there. Reminds me of a story I heard once about a bird who built a perfect nest and wanted to keep it safe. So first she put it in the rice beds, but it got too wet. Then she hid it between rocks, and it was too cold. Then she put it at the top of the tree and it was shaken about by the wind. Then—

—Let me guess. She forgot where her nest was and had to build a whole new one?

Smart ass. Actually, she was too busy worrying about her nest, she forgot to lay any eggs. That was what happened.

She should have just laid her eggs all over the place. Eggs everywhere, man! Like with frogs, they lay trillions of tadpoles, and most get eaten, but some always make it. Or turtles. Just abandon them and some of 'em will make it.

We're not turtles, son. Think about that bird. She wanted things so perfect for her babies. She was so afraid of screwing up, that she screwed up. That's not neglect, it's—

—We're not birds either.

One of the old folk used to talk about that spot, you know. Said it was special because the sun hits the water but the bank is shady. Great for fishing. Although back then they didn't use rods like you got. Those old folk used to set up camp at just the right time of year. Good days and nights, lots of fish and plenty all around to eat. It must have been like a holiday. And later on just one guy would stay back to make sure it was all right. Check the shallows were clear and the trees and bushes were growing well. And make sure all those things got thanked. The fish, the bugs, the breeze—you know the drill. No one left behind.

He'd need to thank the pipe, now. And the pumping stations and leaky valves. The security. Or maybe he would just apologize to the fish. On behalf of all of us down the line driving trucks. Forgive them, fishie, they don't know what they're doing.

That's still a good spot for fishing, with good memories. I remember before that fence went up.

Well, I don't.

Go fishing. You'll remember. It's your job, now, to remember. Go lie down by the bank.

You mean, go trespass. Lie down by some dammed polluted off-limits river.

I mean, remember.

Remember, O LORD, what has befallen us; look, and see our disgrace! Our inheritance has been turned over to strangers, our homes to aliens.

Lamentations 5:1–2

YOSEMITE LAMENTS

Katerina Friesen

O Creator, look and see what has befallen your beloved Ahwahnee!
Remember me. Remember the people who remember my name.
I was hollowed out like a tule reed, trampled down by crowds of foreigners.
Car exhaust chokes my valley, pine beetles gnaw at my drought-
   weakened bark.
Summer fires too-long suppressed turn thick forests to matchsticks,
and winter storms that once blanketed my peaks seldom visit anymore.

Tourists come for "wilderness," land purged of humans,
a park for people to visit but never stay.
These strangers are always on the move, running, restless,
their RVs plastered with my photograph,
looking only through the lens though hardly seeing.
I serve up "nature" for five million a year who drive through,
seeking a place apart from their soiled world.

Of these, there are many who love me, coming from far corners of the
   world,
those who feel Pohono's misty falls touch their cheeks for the first time,
those who stand awestruck in wonder at my sheer cliffs and steep spires,
who delight in each Tuolumne wildflower, pausing, paying attention.
I feel their feet light on my paths, their chalky hands caress my granite faces.
They love me, but most do not know my name.

I remember the people who remember my name,
they who dwelt in me as I dwelt in them:
Ahwahneechee, you exiled ones,
driven out to reservations and scattered
in all directions.
My tears for you are like those streaming
down the face of Tis-sa-ack, the great dome.
I miss your fires that cleared the way for meadow grasses,
burned open land for tender oaks, mule deer, black bear.
Ahwahneechee, the sounds of your grinding stones are heard no more,
gone is the women's laughter as they crushed red manzanita
and pounded fattened acorns from the old black oaks.
Today, food falls to the ground
instead of filling your *chuck-ah* storage and winter bellies.

I taught them my name for 7,000 years—the Paiute,
Miwok, Mono peoples—as they came and went,
trading, dancing, grieving, dying,
birthing, weaving, fishing, singing,
their memories recorded in the rings
of ancient sequoias.

Do you remember, O Creator?
Have you forgotten me?
Have I outlasted you upon this Earth?
You are as slow as the measuring-worm
in its crawl up El Capitan, Tu-Tok-A-Nu'-La!
When will you honour me and those who know my name?
You who delivered Totuya, Maggie Howard, Chief Lemee, Lucy Telles,
bring my people home!
May the crowds of strangers stop and listen,
may you bring their hearts to life like living stones.
Remember me, Ahwahnee, and remember the people
who remember my name.

Restore us that we may be restored;
renew our days as of old.

The hand of the LORD came upon me, and he brought me out by the spirit of the LORD and set me down in the middle of a valley; it was full of bones. He led me all around them; there were very many lying in the valley, and they were very dry. He said to me, "Mortal, can these bones live?" I answered, "O Lord GOD, you know."

Ezekiel 37:1–3

THESE BONES LIVE

Roland Boer

IN NOVEMBER OF 2017, the bones of the oldest human being in Australia were returned to the land from which they came. They travelled from the National Museum of Australia in a hearse to the shores of the now dry, ancient Lake Mungo, in the deserts of Western New South Wales. Once there, they were welcomed by a traditional dance, underwent further rituals of fire, smoke, and words, and were finally returned to the earth. The traditional owners of the land, the Paakantji, Ngyiampaa, and Mutthi Mutthi peoples, oversaw the whole process. For them, the bones had never died. They had come back to tell a story.

In Ezekiel 37, the prophet has a vision of a valley with many bones that are "very dry." Clearly, they have no life in them, for it will require a prophecy to enable them to reassemble, grow sinews, flesh, and skin, before breath can enter them. All of this becomes a parable for the recovery, if not "resurrection" of the people of Israel from exile. To juxtapose this biblical narrative with the story with which I began, instead of bones that need flesh and breath to live, we have living bones that remain bones; in contrast to voice arriving with living breath, the voice emerges through the bones themselves. But in order to see how, I need to tell a little more about the Australian story.

The skeleton in question came to be known as "Mungo Man," due to the location where it was found. It had been "discovered" on Lake Mungo in early 1974 by geologist Jim Bowler and a team of archaeologists. Six years earlier, Bowler had found—some distance away—the bones of a woman who would be called "Mungo Woman" (she was returned to her home in the 1990s). As I indicated earlier, the bones — according to Indigenous people — were not merely "discovered." They had returned to tell a story of their own. And what a story it was and is.

The finds produced a revolution in understanding the history of Aboriginal Australia, for Mungo Man and Mungo Woman were unmistakably Homo Sapiens. Their bones were dated at 42,000 years, almost doubling the previous assumptions concerning how long Indigenous peoples had been in Australia. Subsequent evidence indicates that Aboriginal people and culture have had a continuous presence for 50,000 years. This was a time when Neanderthals still roamed Europe, when megafauna were abundant in Australia, and the inland was moist and lush.

Equally significant was the discovery of burial rites. Mungo Woman's bones had been cremated, crushed, re-burned, and then buried with a coating of ochre (from more than 200 kilometres away). Mungo Man, who died at about 50 years of age and was 170 cm tall, had been stretched out, hands crossed in his lap and his body sprinkled with red ochre. Complex rites and beliefs concerning death undoubtedly accompanied such rituals.

To understand the impact of these discoveries, we need to understand the context. For generations, Settler anthropologists and researchers from around the world sought Australian Indigenous bones since they were believed to represent an earlier and more "primitive" stage in human evolution. Craniums were particularly sought after, given the continuance of "phrenology" until the 1940s. Thousands upon thousands of skeletons were torn from the land and sent to museums in Australia and overseas, without consulting Indigenous peoples. However, Mungo Man and Mungo Woman put an end to any vestiges of "phrenology," or indeed the idea that Indigenous peoples constituted some prior, "primitive" stage. These were modern people, Homo Sapiens, from a very ancient time.

Even more, Mungo Man and Mungo Woman came to play a central role in the rise of recent Aboriginal activism. One dimension of their involvement was in the slogan, "40,000 years is a long, long time; 40,000 years still on my mind." Originally from a song by the influential Joe Geia — a founder of contemporary Indigenous music in Australia — the slogan appeared on a mural in the Redfern Aboriginal community in Redfern, Sydney. It could be seen by anyone entering and leaving Redfern railway station. The consciousness of the sheer length of time, of 10s of millennia, became central to a whole new wave of such activism.

Another dimension of this activism was the drive for the repatriation of the multitude of remains taken from their resting places. This was not merely a valley of bones, but a continent full of bones. Increasingly, the pain for Indigenous peoples became evident, expressed again and again in light of more recent policies that involve consultation at all stages of research. It also became apparent that Indigenous peoples have a profound sense of continuity through the millennia, with a strong responsibility of caring for the ancestors who continued to be present, able to tell their stories to subsequent generations. Over the last few decades, many bones have been returned to their land. But the process is slow and complicated. For example, Mungo Man was formally handed back to the traditional owners in 2015, but his remains were merely shifted from the Australian National University to the museum in the same city, Canberra. A full two years later, Mungo Man finally returned to his resting place.

The bones of Mungo Man and Mungo Woman, along with thousands of other ancestors, are living bones — not dead and dry ones — that returned to teach us something. That return was no accident. The soil around the burial sites eroded for a reason — to show others what the local people had always known, namely, that they had been there from time immemorial. They came back to tell us their stories, the stories of their land and their connection to it. Yes, there have been ruptures in those stories. But this will not destroy the fundamental continuity of the storylines and culture. Moreover, the return of the bones to their land speaks to the recovery of wholeness and continuity, embodied in the need for Indigenous custodianship and care of the land.

The differences between Ezekiel 37 and the Mungo Man and Mungo Woman narratives are clear. And yet the stories come together and touch at another level: through the land. Let me quote two texts to illustrate. The first comes from Ezekiel 37:14: "I will put my spirit within you, and you shall live, and I will place you on your own soil." The second comes from Tanya Charles, a Mutthi Mutthi woman who works at Lake Mungo and was quoted in an article called "Why has it taken so long to repatriate Mungo Man?" She said, "The spirit's always gotta be with the remains. It's very important to be placed in your country and for your spirit to be there."

In Ezekiel 37, God asks the prophet: "Can these bones live?" The answer from Mungo Man and Mungo Woman is clear: these bones live and have a story to tell. The question is whether we will listen.

Nebuchadnezzar said to them, "Is it true, O Shadrach, Meshach, and Abednego, that you do not serve my gods and you do not worship the golden statue that I have set up?"

Daniel 3:14

TRUTH TO POWER

Randy Woodley

PRESIDENT DONALD J. TRUMP made a palatial hotel, trimmed with plated gold, 100 storeys high, complete with a world class golf resort. He set it up next to the plains of the Talladega Superspeedway, near the border of Alabama and Georgia. He then summoned military officers, college and professional sports teams, governors, advisers, state treasurers, judges, senators, congressmen and congresswomen, and all the other U.S. officials to come to the dedication of the resort he had created. So military officers, college and professional sports teams, governors, advisers, state treasurers, judges, senators, congressmen and congresswomen, and all the other U.S. officials assembled for the dedication of the lavish hotel and resort that President Trump had manufactured, and they stood before it.

Then the loud speaker proclaimed, "Peoples of every race and ethnic group, this is what you are to do: As soon as you hear the sound of the 'Star Spangled Banner,' wherever you are, at whatever event, you must stand up, salute the flag, and honour the great things President Trump has done to make America great again, including the work of this spectacular hotel and this world class golf resort. You must pledge loyalty to him and him only. Whoever does not stand up while the national anthem is played and pledge their allegiance to the President for all he has done will immediately be detained and thrown into Rikers Island Prison."

Therefore, as soon as they heard the sound of the "Star Spangled Banner," all peoples of every race and ethnic group stood up facing the American flag that was spread over the hotel. And they acknowledged the great works that President Trump had done to make America great again.

At this time, some Texas Settlers came forward and began denouncing

154

Mexicans. They said to President Trump, "May you be President of these here United States forever! You have issued an order that everyone who hears the sound of the national anthem must stand up and pledge their allegiance to the flag and to you the President, and that whoever does not stand up and pledge their allegiance will be thrown into Rikers Island Prison. But there are some Mexican immigrants who have become citizens — Enrique, Miguel, and Maria — who pay no attention to you, dear President. They neither serve America right by standing for the pledge, nor pledge their allegiance to all you have set up to make America great again."

Burning with rage, President Trump tweeted immediately and summoned Enrique, Miguel and Maria. So these three were brought before the President, who said to them, "Is it true, Enrique, Miguel, and Maria, that you do not stand facing the flag during the national anthem, nor pledge your hearts to all I have set up? Now when you hear the sound of the 'Star Spangled Banner,' if you are ready to stand up and pledge your lives to the flag and to me for all I have done to make America great again, very, very good. But if you do not, you will be thrown into Rikers, a very, very rough place. God help you."

Enrique, Miguel, and Maria replied to him, "President 45, we do not need to defend ourselves before you in this matter. Our citizenship is first to God, then to the Constitution, but not to you and not to the flag. If we are thrown into Rikers Island, the God we serve is able to help us and will deliver us and protect us from your hand. But even if God does not, we want you to know, President 45, that we will not serve you in this way nor acknowledge all you have set up."

President Trump was incensed with Enrique, Miguel, and Maria. He ordered the guards and the prisoners at Rikers to teach them a lesson when they arrived, commanding them to tie up Enrique, Miguel, and Maria and throw them into the hostile prison yard. So these three, wearing only their prison pants and t-shirts, were bound and thrown into the hostile prison yard, which at that time was about to riot. The President's command was so urgent and the prison yard so hostile that some of the prisoners even killed the guards. Yet Enrique, Miguel, and Maria, standing in the midst of hostile prison yard, were not harmed. No one, not one, touched them.

Then President Trump, who was watching this, leapt to his feet in amazement and asked his advisers, "What's happening?! Weren't there three people that we tied up and threw into the prison yard?"

They replied, "Certainly, President Trump."

"Look!" the President exclaimed. "I see four people walking around in the yard, unbound and unharmed, and the fourth looks like an angel!"

President Trump then approached the opening of the prison yard and shouted, "Enrique, Miguel, and Maria, servants of God—the real God—come out!"

So Enrique, Miguel, and Maria came out of the prison yard and the President's advisers crowded around them. They saw that the prisoners had not harmed their bodies, nor was a hair of their heads harmed; their clothes were not dirty or torn, and there was no hint of harm done to them.

President Trump was beside himself. He became quiet. Then, in hushed voice, said, "Praise be to the God of Enrique, Miguel, and Maria. You have sent a deliverer and rescued your servants. They trusted in you and defied my command. They were willing to give up their lives rather than serve any form of power except you, O God. I am humbled before you and realize the error of my ways."

That day, President Trump promoted Enrique, Miguel, and Maria to reform Immigrations and Customs Enforcement policy. He turned his palatial mansion over to the Catholic Workers, who made it a house of hospitality led by the poor. And his golf resort became the biggest community garden the world had seen.

I will restore the fortunes of my
people Israel, and they shall
rebuild the ruined cities and inhabit
them; they shall plant vineyards
and drink their wine, and they shall
make gardens and eat their fruit.

Amos 9:14

A SECURE WORD

Walter Brueggemann

BREAKING NEWS.

From _____ *(name withheld for security reasons) at his home in* _____ *(ditto).*
I was tending my few acres, my neighbours doing the same, when we saw them coming. The hungry ones! Total fear hit—we knew our land rights were in jeopardy. Utter despair struck—for we knew this power, rising on our immediate horizon, was all-consuming. And yet we kept farming. We had no alternative.

But then, beyond our expectation or our understanding, came a voice, crashing in on our anguish. It came through one of our village poets—an authoritative voice, a holy utterance! We knew the poet, yet we did not doubt. This was a sacred word, an assertion from God.

This is what we heard: God addressing us in our despair, God speaking militant words to those who threatened. With care for us peasants, God's going to go after the occupiers! No matter how hard they may try, they cannot hide.

They cannot hide in their racist ideology;
they cannot hide in their technological advantage;
they cannot hide in their enormous power and wealth.

Wherever they might conceal themselves, God will find them out and forcibly turn them back. And God will bring them harm as God brings us peasants good.

The holy voice then declared:

Mighty power will override illusory power!

This God is the God who impinges decisively on human affairs; a God who cannot be prevented from such encroachment. This is the God who governs from on high, who sends rain and drought on our farms. We peasants have always known that. We've always depended on the rain-giving God. But these white occupiers, in their self-deception, have thought otherwise. The God who governs from high above will nullify the dreams of sovereignty made by the colonizers, dreams fuelled by their vaunted technological capacity.

A violent dismantling of imperial power is coming!

The engines of fear will topple;
the economy of exploitative arrogance will fail;
the temples of expansive ideology will be destroyed;
the confiscatory banks will prove empty of power,

all because the holy God will not tolerate such an illusion of self-sufficiency. This God will roll back the abusiveness of colonial exploitation.

And then the poet changed tone. The holy God who addressed threat to invaders turned to reassure me and my peasant neighbours.

God will repair lost villages;
God will recover lost fields;
God will restore the lost resources of our lives.

When we heard these awesome words, we blushed in disbelief. We couldn't imagine such a prospect in our hopelessness. Yet the poet continued:

God's time is coming; the time of the occupiers is over.
God's time will be a time of recovered prosperity for village folk.

Just as greedy agribusiness has disabled the land, so God's new agriculture, managed by peasants like me, recovered acre by acre, will flourish.

The harvest will be so abundant for me and my neighbours that we will be overwhelmed by new crops that keep growing in the recovered land.

We had absolutely nothing to fear. The poet promised—had God promise!—that we would get to keep our land out of the hands of the usurpers.

> We could keep our water and our homes;
> we could work our vineyards and enjoy the wine;
> we could build our small houses and live in them safely;
> we could plant our gardens and enjoy the vegetables.

Our life would be secure. We would be safe from all alarms:

> What have I to dread, what have I to fear,
> leaning on the everlasting arms?
> I have blessed peace with my Lord to trust,
> leaning on the everlasting arms!

Then the poet finished.

We recognized that what we had heard was only human poetry. But, we knew, beyond doubt, this was the utterance of God. It was only a poem, but it changed everything. We knew that the abusive powers would be called to account. We knew that our futures were treasured in the eyes of God. We knew of our worth and our possibility. In response to the hope-filled cadences of the poet, we knew to move beyond fear and despair to courage, energy, and freedom.

> We will keep working our land.
> We will do so unafraid.

He has told you, O mortal, what is good; and what does the LORD require of you but to do justice, and to love kindness, and to walk humbly with your God?

Micah 6:8

WITH MOUNTAINS AND RIVERS BEARING WITNESS

James W. Perkinson

MICAH 6 SLICES the air like lightning: "You have been shown already!"
It is simple. "Do justice. Love kindness. Walk humbly with your God."
But in modern Christianity, we take in the chant with a yawn. Of course.
Just like the love commandment we were taught as kids. As usual — we
ignore context. We swallow platitude. We exit the pew and do like every-
one else. But context is nine-tenths of meaning.

Here the setting is court. Micah is a rustic — a southwest-Ju-
dah-dwelling, out-on-the-land-surviving, lowlands-tempered peasant
(given that his father's name was not recorded and his language is raw
and blunt, it is clear he is not gentry). He faces typical urban predation.
The priests and prophets, as the merchants and judges, are all wheel-
er-dealers with the Powers That Be. Micah rails in crescendoing vibrato
over a rhythm like a drum. He stands as emergency medic and speaks as
prosecutorial griot, announcing coming plague: the advent of sickness,
the revolt of grain and fruit.

> Israel shall eat, but remain hungry;
> farm, but not harvest;
> tread olives and grapes, but neither anoint nor drink.

The polemic target? The hidden hoards of the wealthy, plundered from
the countryside by deceitful business practice, exposed as immoral treasure secured by illegal measure.

The actual law suit? YHWH's own. But it is crucial to hear the roll-call. The court is not human or divine. It is natural. The witnesses summoned are mountains and hills and the "enduring" (a word used for the seventh Hebrew month, so named because the streams "continue to flow") foundations of the earth. The wild heights of Hermon and the perpetual aquifers under the Jordan are the jury. YHWH throws down. Israel has been freed from shackles, brought out of Egypt to re-learn how to live on wild provision in the Sinai outback, brought to the east "gate" of Canaan, where even a "heathen" prophet like Balaam certifies their blessedness—against the designs of his royal employer, Balak. And the conclusion of all of this—a heavy diss of urban life, orchestrated on the back of oppressed labour.

But in particular, Israel is to remember what happened "from Shittim to Gilgal" (Micah 6:5). And here the text can be made to ride heavy on my own situation. I write from the strait (*le détroit*) between Lakes Huron and Erie—the most heavily trafficked commercial border in my country—in a century already fast-becoming the century of Water Wars. Climate change amasses elementary revolt in the form of "water speech," raging in hurricanes and floods, going silent and aloof in drought. As I write, Houston drowns in hurricane Harvey's onslaught—serious, but minor compared to Nigeria, where a large sector is under deluge, or Bangladesh, where one-third of the area is inundated with water and in consequence, has more than 1,200 deaths. Meanwhile, up the road from my crib, 96,000 Flint residents have had their water infrastructure destroyed by state-imposed "emergency manager" incompetence, poisoning children and adults alike.

And my own town continues its draconian practice of emergency management-initiated water shut-offs (more than 100,000 over the last four years) in what looks to be "ethnic cleansing by policy." When considered alongside tax and mortgage foreclosures, and the vacating of one-third of all residences since 2003, the shut-offs of primarily poor people of colour unable to keep up with predatory bank charges and skyrocketing water bills seem a clear bid to re-invent the largest black metropolis in the country as whiter and more upscale.

It's no accident that the city sits on the bank of a river by which 20 percent of the planet's fresh surface water passes (while just north of Flint, Nestlé pumps an aquifer into plastic containers at 200 gallons per

minute in a bottom-line windfall, selling "bottled relief" to groups trying to address the immediate crisis). Water is clearly the premium wild
power now targeted for enslavement and use by the corporate elites to
secure profit and large-living on Indigenous land and the backs of the
oppressed.

"Doing justice," "loving with steadfastness," and "walking as a little one concerned for other little ones" has meant, for this wanna-be
Christian author, engaging in direct action, with a "Water Warrior" co-
hort of African American crones and hip-hop heads, mobilizing grass
roots efforts to try to throw a Micah-like "monkey wrench" into busi-
ness-as-usual. And in the process, learning from contemporary Ojibwa
Water Walkers (around the Great Lakes) and Three Fires Dwellers on the
Bend, that water is not mere resource, but Living Being, with Whom we
must relate in symbiosis and to Whom we owe ritual gift and gratitude!

Against such a backdrop, consider the deep meaning of the "steadfast
loving" Micah counselled in his day. At issue is *hesed*—in Hebrew, a
word for how well Israel keeps the "original instructions"—the covenant relation with YHWH-Elohim, enjoined from the beginning.
That covenant was enacted by means of rain-cloud signs given to Noah
(Genesis 9:8–17), animal blood offered by Abraham (sacrificed not
just to pleasure God's inhaling nostrils, but also to be eaten as provision; Genesis 15:7–21), and later re-convened by Hosea in a wilderness
tryst, abolishing war and embracing beast, bird, and ground-creeping
soil-worker, promising rain, grain, wine, and oil (Hosea 2:18–23). All
which is to say, "steadfast love" references

wild dove,
pastoral herd,
sprouting seed,
mountain rock,
nutrient-rich soil, and
flowing river.

It has never been only about "God" and "human."

And for Micah, as for here and now, a primal focus must be "what
happened between Shittim and Gilgal" (Micah 6:5). The Israelites—on-
the-run ex-slaves re-learning the land—crossed the river. Water politics

was central to their success on the Amorite land just east of the Jordan ford; Moses provided them drink by means of digging a well called Beer (so they did not need to encroach on the well commandeered by a hostile king; Numbers 21:16–18, 21–22). Like any well-versed Bedouin crew, they did not merely lap up the gift, but sang to it—as if water was a living creature. As indeed, it is.

Walking away from urban temptations, marketed by the king of Moab to leverage curse on the crowd (Numbers 25), they passed through the life-blood of the region, the Jordan, gift from mountain heights of Hermon to the north (Joshua 3:1–5:12)—the very source and substance of the "on-high" blessing Balaam promised in spite of himself (Numbers 2:41; 23:3, 9, 13–14, 27–28). Entering as Settlers onto the lands of others, they had the "humble sense" to enter covenant-parity with those on the West Bank who had already exited empire's Mediterranean-seaboard cities and re-learned the land in small-scale horticultural interdependence with soil-riches and rain-gifts (rather than trying to reproduce the high-tech irrigation-trenches of Mesopotamia and the forced labour camps of Egypt).

Early Israel was actually an amalgam of escaped-slaves-become-nomad herders and renegade-peasants-become-native farmers. Only later would Israel opt for monarchy and create the need for prophetic throw-down like Micah's. Would that my own colonizing people had entered such an Indigenously-influenced amalgam! But we have needed Micah from the beginning. And so, even this late in the game: do justice, love steadfastness, and walk humbly, indeed.

In the time of King Herod, after Jesus was born in Bethlehem of Judea, wise men from the East came to Jerusalem, asking, "Where is the child who has been born king of the Jews? For we observed his star at its rising, and have come to pay him homage."

Matthew 2:1—2

WORD OF LIBERATION

Peter C. Phan

THE STORIES NARRATED in Matthew 2:1–23 could be easily dismissed in our day as "fake news" or "alternative facts." Is it true that Magi from the East travelled to Jerusalem to find the "king of the Jews"? Is it true that Jesus was born in Bethlehem under threat of death? Is it true that the Holy Family fled to Egypt to escape Herod's massacre of the innocents?

For many historians, the fact that these stories are reported only by Matthew, without mention anywhere else in the New Testament, casts serious doubt on their historical authenticity. Moreover, the miraculous elements that suffuse the stories—the star which reveals the birth of the newborn king and guides the Magi to the very place where Jesus is to be found; dreams as means of divine communication; angelic visitations—are the stuff of legend and not historiographical data. Even the Magi—well-attested historical figures in Persia, Babylon, and Arabia, variously described as magicians, astrologers, and Zoroastrian priests—seem to function in this narrative as religious symbols rather than flesh-and-blood persons.

Some biblical scholars reckon that such arguments do not discredit Matthew 2's historicity, or at least, its probability. The text refers to well-known historical figures such as Herod, the chief priests, the teachers of the law, and Archelaus, as well as identifiable geographical areas such as Judea (Judah), Jerusalem, Bethlehem, Egypt, Ramah, and Nazareth. Yet given its mélange of ostensibly legendary materials and historical facts, most regard Matthew 2 as "midrash," a literary genre that attempts to comment on and interpret a biblical text by means of other writings, or by telling stories that may or may not be true to reveal deeper meanings.

While the historical-critical method of reading the Bible is indispensable for sorting facts from myth in the scriptures — albeit rarely yielding apodictic certainty — it is by no means the only hermeneutical tool, nor the most helpful way for contemporary readers to discern the biblical message guiding their lives. With the historical-critical method, we engage the Bible like a window; we can look behind it to discover what really happened — the world "behind" the text. Yet the Bible also conveys God's message for our salvation and serves us much like a mirror; we can look into it and see ourselves enacted in the biblical story and addressed by God's word — the world "in/of" the text. And importantly, the Bible is also like God's beckoning voice. It opens up a new way of being and living in the world, a way that God's grace empowers us to humbly and boldly perform — the world "in front of" the text.

When read in these second and third ways, the stories narrated in Matthew 2 can no longer be rejected as "fake news" like they might be in our contemporary socio-political milieu. Rather, they function as God's radical call to seek justice and hunger for liberation. Specifically, they function as God's summons to struggle alongside all those threatened with mass state violence, the politically and religiously persecuted, and those forced to flee their homelands.

Take and read the midrash of Matthew 2 once again. Can you see it?

Note how the Magi asked the people of Jerusalem about "the one who has been born king of the Jews." By using "king" three times in the first three verses, once for Jesus and twice for Herod, Matthew wants to draw our attention to this title, "king of the Jews." It was this title that Herod claimed for himself. Consider the irony.

Herod was *made* king of the Jews by the Roman senate; he bought his kingship by acting in the interests of the Roman Empire, thus serving his own desires and well-being over-against those of his people. Herod was therefore an illegitimate client-king. By contrast, Jesus was *born* king of the Jews. His kingship is his natural heritage; he is the Son of David, having been born in Bethlehem in Judah, the city of David.

Like all dictators, Herod stopped at nothing to preserve his power, which could only survive by dint of lies, torture, and murder — even the slaughter of children. Jesus, on the other hand, was "a ruler who will shepherd" God's people as the Good Shepherd, that is, one who would go to the uttermost lengths to care for the beloved community—even to the point of laying down his life.

Today, every Christian, like the Magi, is challenged to discern the difference between these two kinds of political leaders—be they pharaoh, king or queen, president or prime minister. Today, every Christian is called by Matthew's courageous midrash to stand up to those who act like King Herod, to speak truth to power in the name of Jesus, the king of the Jews, in solidarity with the blessed "wretched of the earth."

At present, over three percent of the current world population—more than 240 million persons—are migrants. It's an astounding number that has led some to dub our current epoch the "Age of Migration." There are, of course, many kinds of migrants, yet the largest number are economic migrants. In search of job opportunities, many poor go abroad, the majority of whom are women often subjected to physical violence and sexual abuse, and frequently exploited by their own governments and corporations. Yet the most tragic migrants might be, like the Holy Family, forced migrants.

Of the 65 million displaced people in today's world, more than 25 million of them are refugees. Waves upon waves of refugees have recently been cast out of their homes in the Middle East, Myanmar, Central Africa, and Central America because of war and unspeakable violence. And sadly, they often have nowhere to settle. Like the Holy Family—who were forced to relocate to Nazareth, well over 100 kilometers away from their familiar neighbourhood of Bethlehem—they cannot return to their homes, which have been taken over by their enemies or destroyed.

Right now, a catastrophic war is being waged that is creating a new breed of forced migrants. It is the assault against the earth that goes under the innocuous handle of "global warming." In places such as the Maldives, Kiribati, the Solomon Islands, Fiji, and Cape Verde, millennia-old homelands are being threatened or submerged by rising sea levels. Peoples who are not responsible for the creation crisis are bearing the climate cross that has been manufactured by major greenhouse gas emitters. Some have had to flee as their countries experience grave dangers to their communal well-being and their social and personal identities, not to mention their statehood and citizenship. And in the years ahead, hundreds of thousands will be forced to do the same.

As global warming displaces and disinherits the poor, a dramatic surge of xenophobia, racism, anti-immigrant policy, and Islamophobia has swept across the globe and captured the hearts and minds of supposedly Christian nations, including the United States of America, England, Germany, Italy, Hungary, and Poland. Can the subversive memories of Matthew 2 speak truth into this capricious situation?

As I brood over these gospel stories, somehow I can hear the Spirit say: "In the name of Jesus, Mary, and Joseph, in the name of the forced and returning migrants, in the name of the children who are massacred by the murderous Herods in so many lands, all you Christians of conscience rise up! Rise and resist the crushing greed, bloodshed, and callous indifference of the Powers That Be! Rise up, with tears and bold lament, and warn your wayward Christian family who have embraced the wide path of destruction! Rise and resist all those who support violent policies of exclusion and anxious self-interest! Repent and find the better way! For unless you welcome the stranger, the God of Jesus—the God of the Paradigmatic Migrant—will rise up against you on the Last Day!"

These ancient gospel stories are no joke. They offer profound challenge and have the ability to unsettle our certitudes. Recall the witness of the Magi. Whoever they may be—astrologers, magicians, wise men, Zoroastrian priests, or court counsellors—one thing is certain. They are non-Jews. The *goyim*. The "pagans" and "heathens" whom Christian tradition has long condemned to hell for their lack of faith. But here they are: they are the first to see the star of Jesus at its rising in the East; they are gutsy, risk-taking people of faith who act on their discovery by undertaking an arduous journey to find this king of the Jews; they are people of costly devotion, for having found the Christ, they prostrate and worship him with gifts of considerable worth—gold, frankincense, and myrrh. They are Christian *avant la lettre*. Christians before there were Christians.

Revelation 3:22 says, "Whoever has ears, let them hear what the Spirit says to the churches." To some, Matthew 2 is "fake news" and a set of "alternative facts." But if we take the text seriously and read it as holy midrash, if we open our hearts to hear the Spirit address our world and our own deepest selves, we can discover a living word of liberation, a word from God.

In those days, John the Baptist appeared in the wilderness of Judea, proclaiming, "Repent, for the kingdom of heaven has come near."

Matthew 3:1–2

THE FIRE OF KISEMANITO

Mark Bigland-Pritchard

JUST GOING ON vision quest wasn't enough for Johnny. The boreal forest was where he encountered Creator and heard the truths that his people needed to hear. He couldn't return to the routine of community life after that.

Johnny avoided the best hunting grounds in his peoples' territory. He lived off nuts and berries instead, and sometimes he would find a bees' nest and take some of the honey. It wasn't much, but he didn't need much. He mostly needed that connection with Creator.

From time to time he would come back to the reserve, or to the city, and he would rant. You couldn't hear him without feeling just a little bit smaller — sometimes a great deal smaller. And yet he had something that made you want to listen. Something to do with authenticity. You knew that he was speaking truth, and you had to respond to it.

Johnny told people to turn away from their bad habits and bad attitudes, and to return to Creator's original instructions. He told them that Creator would be bringing in a new order, and that they needed to get ready.

Anyone who listened to him and took his message to heart, anyone who chose to leave behind their bad habits and bad attitudes, would smudge with sage and partake in a purification ceremony along the banks of the Missinipiy.

Johnny expected people to mean what they said. He didn't think much of people who just did ceremony for show. So, when some of the politicians started asking if they could join the ceremony, and some false spiritual leaders showed up (with their desire to control), Johnny was angry. "Who told you devouring spirits to come? Did Witiko send you? Who warned you of the consequences of your corruption?

"Show that you have changed, and then you can come back," he demanded. "It's not good enough to say that you belong to Kisemanito's people—these rocks could speak for the nation if Kisemanito so desires. You are like Saskatoon bushes that bring forth no berries: and if you don't change, you'll be cut down and burnt.

"I use water and medicines in my purification ceremonies. But there is a greater and more powerful one coming soon, and he won't need those things. He will have the Spirit of Kisemanito, and he will purify with the fire of Kisemanito. That fire will consume everything that is rotten inside you, but anything that is good will survive."

Give us this day our daily bread. And forgive us our debts, as we also have forgiven our debtors.

Matthew 6:11–12

YOU AND MADRE TIERRA

Rose Marie Berger

"AND WHEN YOU talk to Creator, do not be like those whose prayers are like pine splinters, wheedling under the skin, for they only know conniving; they strap empty words to stone buildings and creeds, seeking to prop up their own spirits, which are as weak as badly mixed mortar poured in winter. It will neither set nor hold a foundation. Their temples will fall down, their beliefs will run out.

"But whenever you talk to Creator, burn a little copal, set out a bowl of water, and some salt and honey, then sing a little song to the four directions to let God know you are there. In this way, Creator comes quietly to you, like a hummingbird dancing on the scent of sweet flowers. And Creator will release to you what is needed. You do not need market-words to buy and sell God's favour. You don't need shoes, or books, or prayer cards. Creator is listening. Pray this way."

¤

In a small house in Hillandale, Maryland, between the Capital Beltway and the Anacostia River, a family of Indigenous Salvadorans blessed their evening meal. Margarito Esquino prayed the Lord's prayer in his native Nahua:

Tat nupal tey tinemi tic ne ylhuicatl.

Rough hands gripped mine. Seven stood around a yellow-silver Formica table heavy with pupusas, butter, corn, queso fresco, and Kool-Aid in plastic cups.

Our Creator in the sky and Mother Earth.

I stared down, uncomfortable. I was their guest. Spanish was their second language, their bondage language. Anglo-English my first, with hopscotch Spanish (hop from noun to verb) a very distant second. I clung to the edges of Nahua, its narrow tones and rhythm like wind, hovering.

Margarito Esquino and Maria Mendez Esquino fled their traditional lands in what is now called the region of Sonsonate, El Salvador. Margarito was the son of the spiritual leader Chief Adrian Esquino Lisco. In Chief Adrian's youth, more than 32,000 Indigenous people were killed in "La Matanza," a 1932 military campaign meant to exterminate El Salvador's native population, particularly the Nahuatl, Lenca, and Maya communities.

In 1954, Margarito's grandfather founded the Asociación Nacional Indígena Salvadoreña. They were Nahuatl, Lenca, and Maya weavers; fisherfolk running a small shrimp cooperative, and farmers with several sites owned cooperatively.

¤

"Creator is listening to you: 'Our Creator in the sky, we kiss the earth before you. You order our steps, our fields, our days and nights. Today you gave us good maize for cornmeal and beautiful corn plants that make our hearts glad. When we sell ourselves or allow ourselves to be bought, we ask that you not demand too great a sacrifice from us to restore us to justice. Tomorrow we will make it right. Protect us from the one who sows borers in our crops and fear in our family. Protect us from the men with guns. For you are our Creator. All we have is you and Madre Tierra where we stand."

¤

In 1983, paramilitaries attacked again. The Las Hojas cooperative members received death threats, were brutally beaten, and had their homes destroyed by bulldozers; women and children were beaten and raped.

Maria and Margarito fled north, secured "refugee" status in what is now the United States, and were charged by Margarito's father to provide for the safety, well-being, and right to practice Indigenous cultural traditions of the Nahuatl, Lenca, and Maya diaspora in the U.S.

In Maryland, Margarito worked construction. Maria cleaned offices and a church. They offered ceremony for those who requested it. Their small house, between the Capital Beltway and the Anacostia River, was in the traditional territory of the Piscataway Nation. As Nahuatl tribal leaders, Margarito and Maria were welcomed by Chief Billy Tayac, traditional elder for the Piscataway. Members of Asociación Nacional Indigena Salvadoreña held ceremonies for their youth on Piscataway lands. Gifts were exchanged. Sweats were held—even a Sun Dance.

Pray this way and Madre Tierra will rejoice with you.

As for me, I am still their guest—as I have been for the past 300 years when my ancestors arrived in the Carolinas as refugees, fleeing men with guns intent on enclosing the communal lands and clearing the Scottish Highlands. My language, even my prayers, are guests.

He answered, "It is not fair to take the children's food and throw it to the dogs." She said, "Yes, Lord, yet even the dogs eat the crumbs that fall from their masters' table."

Matthew 15:26–27

TALKING BACK: A SERMON

Julia M. O'Brien

IT'S HARD TO FIND a place to stand in Matthew's story of the Canaanite woman, a vantage point from which to hear his testimony as good news. It's always tempting to stand with Jesus. To walk with him. To want to be like him. But the story makes it difficult to want to do what Jesus did, for he does not embrace the Canaanite woman or treat her with dignity.

When Jesus comes to her town and she calls out, "Have mercy on me, Lord, Son of David; my daughter is tormented by a demon," he doesn't even acknowledge her. When the disciples goad him to send her away, he finally speaks, but only to refuse her. "I was sent only to the lost sheep of the house of Israel." Jesus' healing apparently isn't for those outside his circle, even when he is a guest in their land. When she kneels and begs him for help, he doesn't just repeat his refusal. He throws in an insult, comparing her—or maybe her daughter—to a dog. "It isn't fair to take children's food and throw it to the dogs."

Perhaps you've heard preachers defend Jesus' comparison, who claim the Greek (*kynaria*) actually refers not to a stray dog but a household pet, a puppy. Perhaps you've heard teachers explain Jesus' actions as simply a test of the woman's faith, to see if she really meant it.

That's all wrongheaded. And dangerous. Comparing a woman to a dog was not a compliment in the ancient world any more than it is on today's social media. Demeaning someone's ethnicity was no more affectionate in the ancient world than it is on the streets of present-day Charlottesville, embattled by white nationalism. As to the testing, nobody else in the Gospel of Matthew gets tested like this, not even the other Gentile characters. When a Roman centurion comes to Jesus a few chapters earlier and asks for the healing of his slave, Jesus simply says, "I will come and cure him." No slurs about his ethnicity. No comment on his role as occupier of Judea. No test to see how much he really wanted his slave to be healed—or why.

Matthew's testimony doesn't make me want to stand with Jesus in this encounter. I know where I want to stand: with the Canaanite woman. Even in the moment of denigration, this woman is clever enough to turn Jesus' comparison against him. "Even the dogs get something," she says. "Compare me to a dog if you want, but at least give me a scrap." Like a voice from the Psalms, she accepts her lowly estate but calls the divine one to be consistent. "I am a worm, but save me, Holy One."

For decades, feminist interpreters of this story have argued that she is not only persistent but also persuasive; that she changes Jesus and the trajectory of the gospel; that her faith is so powerful she converts Jesus to the Gentile mission. I wish that were Matthew's testimony, but I don't think it is. Jesus had already praised the faith of other Gentiles, like the centurion, without being changed. And after the encounter with the Canaanite woman, women get more silent in the gospel of Matthew, not more empowered. She gets healing for her daughter, but the structures of Matthew—the structures of the world—don't change.

However, there is danger in assuming that I stand in the Canaanite woman's place, that she and I are the same. As Musa Dube insists, when white women erase a person's ethnicity to identify with her gender, they show themselves blind to their own privilege. This character isn't just a woman, but a Canaanite woman—one who has had to endure not only sexism but also her people's loss of their ancestral land and the religious justifications for that land seizure. When I claim her testimony as just-like-mine, I become like women from the United States who visit the Two-Thirds world and see only women victimized by patriarchy, rather than women who are victimized by the economic and governmental policies that support my home ownership and my retirement fund. When I claim her testimony as just-like-mine, I ignore the brutal settler colonial history of these United States, in which white Christian peoples displaced and slaughtered Indigenous peoples whom they compared to Canaanites.

As much as I prefer otherwise, Matthew's story places those like me in the role not of characters within the story, but as bystanders who are publicly confronted with this larger-than-life monument to abuse. And, as with other monuments of violence, we are put into the position of having to decide what to do with it.

Will we simply ignore this episode and cross the street to another Scripture passage that will feel more comfortable? Will we do some revisionist history, to make the story okay, as a way of protecting the reputation of our beloved founder, Jesus? Will we explain this away as something that only happened in the past, something we congratulate ourselves for moving beyond?

Here's my proposal. Let's put this monument in a newly-constructed community center, alongside other monuments of oppression. In front of this monument will be a stage and an open mic, and folks will be invited to stand there and tell their stories — of abuse inflicted from the outside by those who can only see their otherness, and abuse inflicted on the self by having to accept mistreatment in order to beg for what has been freely offered to others.

I imagine that we'll hear from LGBTQ2 folks who have had to endure their own version of "dog" slurs and reasoned arguments from religious leaders, forced to beg for inclusion into Jesus' church. I imagine that we'll hear from persons of colour who endure racist remarks and the denigration of their sources of wisdom in order to succeed in white dominant institutions. I imagine that Indigenous peoples, made invisible by overwhelming forces of assimilation and genocide, will be represented in abundance. And I imagine that there will be yet other stories from those whom the structures of this world keep on the margins, forever Canaanites.

In the middle of the room there will be a table filled with all the bounties of the earth. Lots of kale. And bread and wine. There will be enough for everyone, so that no one has to beg for the crumbs that fall to the floor. And around that table we will share stories of where we have found healing and how we might help others find it as well.

As for a name, I propose we call this community centre "church." Our logo will not be the monument itself, but an image of people talking back to the monument. And we can use this motto: "what has been is not what must be."

And Jesus came and said to them, "All authority in heaven and on earth has been given to me. Go therefore and make disciples of all nations, baptizing them in the name of the Father and of the Son and of the Holy Spirit."

Matthew 28:18–19

RESISTING THE GREAT CO-MISSION

Mitzi J. Smith

IN THE AGE of imperialism, a tragedy of the so-called *Great Commission* occurred—the collusion of Church and Crown. Together, the two—*a great co-mission*—went forth in God's name

> To conquer and expand
>> territories and holdings
> To deplete and ravish
>> land, resources, and peoples
> To do great things for God and/as King

>> an uncivilized taming

> It was a great co-mission
>> of evangelicalism and colonial politics
>>> a co-constitutive relationship
>> a devastation
>> a genocide
>>> of non-white Indigenous people
>>> of God's children
>>> children of the global south

Who christened them and it—Matthew 28:16–20—as the *Great Commission*, knowing it was a *great co-mission*, a sacralization of evil? In the 1700s, Crown and Church coined the phrase.

It covered a multitude of sins
Prioritizing gospel teaching
      to others
      other peoples
      other nations
"Hastening" the second coming of Jesus
      the apocalyptic end of time
      bringing non-white Indigenous peoples to
      their Jesus through
      their gospel
      by any means necessary

            forced conversions
            threats of death
            "slaves obey your masters"
            demonizing cultures
                  no dancing, no "magic," no "conjuring"
                  no Swahili or native tongues
                  no Supreme God that we did not name

The white, blue-eyed Jesus
Behold your God!
      by any means necessary
            removing children from their homes
            depositing them in boarding schools
                  a great miseducation
            raping people and land
            in the name of the cloroxed Christ

The *great co-mission*
      masqueraded as good news
      refusing to disrobe
            to be exposed for what it was and is
            to be found guilty before God
      insisting upon the superiority of the white race
      asserting the inferiority of non-white peoples
      sanctifying themselves the only legitimate teachers

and others as their students
whole nations constructed as ignorant pagans
neglecting the greater things of God

love
divine love for all God's children
Indigenous self-love
neighbour love
setting the captives free
healing damaged hearts
eliminating poverty

Today, a restless ghost from the past haunts us, characterized by this same intersectionality of religion, white nationalism, and neo-colonialism. Our current President of the United States campaigned on the mantra "Make America Great Again." White conservative evangelicals, 82 percent of whom voted for that demagogue, zealously embrace this noxious slogan. These make-America-great-again evangelicals

Anoint Trump as the world's saviour
Pray for his/their pro-white
anti-foreigner, anti-immigrant, anti-gay, anti-intellectual,
anti-living wage, anti-women's rights, anti-gun control,
anti-global warming, anti-BlackLivesMatter, anti-#MeToo
agenda

Like the white backlash against Reconstruction after the emancipation of enslaved Africans, white supremacists fight

To maintain white privilege
symptomatic of systemic racism and sexism
sentimental for the days BEFORE
a black president
a burgeoning non-white, immigrant population
gay rights
Roe v. Wade
Brown v. Board of Education

For missionaries of conservative white Christianity, President Trump is a Messiah-figure. "I think evangelicals have found," said Jerry Falwell Jr., "their dream President."

Like missionaries of the so-called *Great Co-mission*, the disciples of the *neo-colonial-great co-mission* see themselves as doing great things for their God. They have partnered with a capitalist, warmongering, p*ssy-grabbing, and Bible-(mis)quoting bully. And like the missionaries of the earlier *great co-mission*, today's neo-colonial co-missionaries assume a white supremacist legacy and a white nationalist agenda that prioritizes the spread of their truth disguised as God's good news through their consecrated white messengers.

In the eyes of those missionaries, they are the authentic successors to the poor, colonized, Jewish Palestinian peasants that lived under the gaze and mighty hand of Roman imperial power. But context matters! Jesus' instructions to his disciples were antithetical to empire and neo-colonialism. Jesus said take nothing for your journey and graciously receive the hospitality of your neighbours (Matthew 10:10). But the *co-missionaries* of the *Great Co-mission* took advantage of their neighbours' hospitality. It was the Indigenous peoples, not the missionaries, who needed to shake the dust off their feet because of the missionaries' perversion of God's good news.

Most non-whites resisted and continue to resist the dominant reading of Matthew 28 that understands the white man as "ye" and all others as the nations to whom "ye" was/are sent. They resisted in the 1700s and they resist today. Some have rejected the gospel of the white man *and* his Bible outright. Others reinterpret the Bible in ways that reflect their God-experience and God-knowledge. Some have decided that ordaining Matthew 28:16–20 as the *great commission* doesn't reflect the crux of the gospel.

Our greatest calling is not to "go out and teach others," but to love ourselves while we love others. The greatest command, according to Jesus, is to love God and to love our neighbours as we love ourselves (Matthew 22:37–39). One of the greatest acts of resistance for oppressed and marginalized peoples is the act of self-love and self-care. We were taught to hate ourselves and our cultures. But we must love ourselves well—to unabashedly affirm our self-dignity—so we can love others well. In the name of love, we reject white supremacy, white nationalism, xenophobia, homophobia, p★ssy-grabbers, racism, sexism, and ableism. We reclaim our voices, our love of self, and our inestimable worth. We affirm with so many black women participants in the modern civil rights movement that "from one blood God made all nations to inhabit the earth" (Acts 17:26).

The beginning of the good
news of Jesus Christ, the Son
of God. As it is written in the
prophet Isaiah, "See, I am sending
my messenger ahead of you, who
will prepare your way; the voice of
one crying out in the wilderness:
'Prepare the way of the Lord, make
his paths straight.'"

Mark 1:1–3

A SHAMAN APPEARED IN VENTURA

Ched Myers

A CRITICAL TASK for today's church is to take up a "re-placed the-ology." That is, to reclaim symbols of redemption that are Indigenous to the bioregion in which the church dwells, to remember the stories of the peoples of the land, and to sing anew its old songs. These can then be woven together with the symbols, stories and songs of biblical radicalism.

I live and work in Oak View, California, the Ventura River Watershed. This is traditional territory of the Chumash people, with stories that go back millennia. How might I transpose the history, culture and land-scape of the gospel story onto this context, so that I can become more attentive to, and literate in, the deep social history and ecology of each? The following is an effort to re-narrate Mark's portrait of John the Baptist (1:1–9) amongst the Chumash in the mid-19th century. It is excerpted from a longer, fuller treatment of Mark's prologue (1:1–18).

VERSE 1. *Here's how the "Good Way" of Jesús was rediscovered and passed on to another generation.*

I use the Spanish Jesús to acknowledge the colonial substrate of my historical and geopolitical context. Much of the Ventura Watershed is mountainous and still largely uninhabited, framed by the Santa Ynez and the Topa Topa ranges (Spanish and Chumash names). The Chumash are the First Peoples, a thriving and sustainable hunter-gatherer, seafar-ing, and complex culture until successive and brutal waves of Spanish (1769–1820), Mexican (1820–48), and American (1848–present) colonization. They survive in small numbers, and, though they are not a federally recognized tribe, Chumash leaders persist in the long, slow struggle to rebuild their language, ceremonies, identity, and roles as traditional stewards of this land.

For my recontextualization, I choose a crucial point in the mid-19th century process of colonization in southern California as a temporal setting. On the eve of the U.S. takeover of California in 1848 (as part of the spoils of the Mexican-American war at the Treaty of Guadalupe Hidalgo), the situation of the Chumash was dire. Settlers had driven most from their traditional villages and hunting grounds, and those who had been taken into the Mission system were largely abandoned after Mexican secularization in 1833. With neither treaties nor reservations, disease, dispossession, and slavery had taken a huge toll—though things would get much worse under American rule.

VERSES 2–3. *As was depicted in ancient cave paintings by the Old Ones, a shaman would appear in the backcountry of Ventura. He would be called by the Spirit to discover a new Rainbow Bridge for the People to cross to regain their health and freedom.*

There are many surviving pictograph sites throughout this terrain, believed to have been created by shamanic leaders; these are sacred to the Chumash, thus analogous to the Jewish scriptures Mark cites. The "Rainbow Bridge" is a Chumash creation/migration story. Hutash (Earth Mother) grew the People from magic seeds she planted on Limuw (Santa Cruz Island). But when it got too crowded, Hutash created a tall spanning bridge from a *wishtoyo* (a rainbow) for the people to walk across to the mainland. They migrated over the bridge to the Ventura and Santa Barbara areas, but some fell off into the ocean and became dolphins, whom the Chumash honour as relatives.

I am using this myth as a "new start" archetype comparable to Mark's notion of repentance (Gk. *metanoia*) as "turning around and heading in a new direction." The journey motif echoes Mark's invocation of the Exodus journey as the Way of Discipleship.

VERSE 4. *Kitsepawit came down from Iwihinmu. He began telling his people that the project of European colonization was all wrong and that the Great*

Spirit wanted to bring back the Old Ways. He invited them into a water ritual that signalled an intent to "turn things around."

At 8,847 feet, Iwihinmu (Mt. Pinos) is the highest point in Ventura County. Considered by the Chumash to be the centre of the world where everything is in balance, its summit lies at the heart of their traditional territory.

In response to 19th-century colonialism, native renewal movements often arose, frequently led by Indigenous prophets; the Ghost Dance in the American prairies during the 1890s is perhaps the most well-known example. I have imagined such a movement among the Chumash, though in fact there were only a few native revolts in southern California during the first 75 years of European colonization, and none was dramatically successful. Two of note were in 1785, led by a Tongva female shaman, Toypurina, and the 1824 Chumash revolt at Santa Barbara (the state's largest on record). But most Chumash in the central coast region survived through assimilation.

Taking my cue from Mark's prologue, however, I imagine a "John the Baptist" type figure sparking a movement of Chumash renewal and resistance, drawing an analogy between first-century Jews (the principle "neo-Indigenous" population in Palestine) under Roman occupation, and 19th-century Chumash under Mexican/American occupation. (John was recognized by Herodean authorities as a dissident, and eventually arrested and executed.) I have chosen Fernando Librado Kitsepawit (1839–1915) as a "prophetic" figure, not because he played that role historically, but because we know a great deal about him (relative to most other 19th-century Chumash), as he was a major cultural informant to ethnographer John Harrington in 1912.

Kitsepawit's parents were brought from Santa Cruz Island as children to Mission San Buenaventura and married in 1830. Kitsepawit was raised at the Mission but lived much of his later life on ranches to the north. He was fluent in Spanish and English and knew how to read and write (his later-adopted name, Librado, means "book lover"). Though not a traditional shaman, Kitsepawit was literate in Chumash ritual, voyaging, and song.

Having witnessed the breakdown of the mission communities and the influx of American Settlers, Kitsepawit survived on the margins of society, like most Chumash during this period. He often lived in a cave while working at local ranches and was known to have spent consider-able time in the backcountry of Ventura and Santa Barbara, gathering food and plant medicine.

VERSE 5. *Chumash and others caught in the Mission system went out to Kitsepawit. They came from all over southern California. A few Settlers too, even all the way from the big pueblo of San Francisco. They came for his purification ceremony in Matilija Creek up in the mountains, washing the colonial civiliza-tion right off and out of them.*

In my re-imagining, Kitsepawit sparks a movement with a water rit-ual — traditionally used by Chumash healers for purification ceremo-nies — in Matilija Creek (a Chumash name of unknown meaning), one of the tributaries of the Ventura River. Because it is hidden away up in rugged mountain canyons, it would have been an ideal place for a native resistance movement. (Local lore claims that the notorious Mexican social bandit Joaquin Murrieta hid out there, where today there is a Murrieta Trail).

By the 1840s, the closest Chumash villages of Matilija and Ojai had been depopulated. Refugees from there and from San Buenaventura Mission built traditional *aps* (brush huts) near the mouth of the Ojai valley near Cañada Larga, close to a sacred sycamore tree, at the site of a Mission *Asistencia* (outlying chapel) not far from the Ventura River. While this would be a lovely site for my imagined baptism, it would have been too visible and vulnerable to the colonizers.

Los Angeles would have been the closest major pueblo, but the growing city of San Francisco would more accurately be the equivalent of Jerusalem in Mark's narrative, the political and socio-economic cap-ital of Judea.

VERSE 6. *Now Kitsepawit was naked except for a loincloth, as in the old ways, and he ate acorns and chia, hunted squirrels and fished. He sang old songs.*

Acorns, chia seed (from sage) and small game were staples of the Chumash diet. Kitsepawit seems to have practised some of the old ways. American Settler John Begg recollected that, "His cave was a little distance from the school.... That was where he kept his blankets, where he slept.... He used to travel all up through the hills here to get herbs for medicine." Alongside the gathering of traditional foods, Kitsepawit would have practised traditional songs. In 1913, he was recorded singing a customary song from the Santa Cruz Island Chumash.

VERSES 7 –9. *Kitsepawit would paint in his cave and kept saying that another prophet was coming who was even wiser and more powerful, and that he was just apprenticing to that one. "I have cleansed you with water," he said, "but the coming one will purify you with Creator's Spirit." After a while a man named Jesús canoed in from Wi'ma, and he was immersed by Kitsepawit down into the creek there at the foot of the mountains.*

I chose Wi'ma (Santa Rosa Island) as Jesús' "home" because, as an off-shore island, it was out of the way and relatively ignored by the colonizers (like Nazareth). Archaeologists have found the oldest human remains in North America there, pre-dating the Aleutian land bridge by several thousand years (suggesting that the Chumash may have arrived originally by sea—Polynesia?). *Tomols* (traditional plank canoes) played an important role in the 1824 Chumash revolt at Santa Barbara. Today, the modern Chumash Maritime Society paddles to Limuw (Santa Cruz Island) to perform ceremony, and in so doing, honours the dignity, identity, and survival of the Chumash.

¤

How might *you* renarrate this gospel episode in terms of your own bioregion? Which places in your watershed might be analogous to Mark's wilderness, or to the Jordan River? What historical dynamics of power and social crisis in your context might resemble Mark's geo-political specificity, in which native inhabitants suffering under foreign domination were drawn out to the margins to encounter a wilderness prophet? In working with this exercise, both ancient text and our social and ecological context spring to life through analogical imagination. This can help us decolonize scripture, its interpretation, and our own contexts.

A leper came to him begging him, and kneeling he said to him, "If you choose, you can make me clean." Moved with pity, Jesus stretched out his hand and touched him, and said to him, "I do choose. Be made clean!"

Mark 1:40–41

MENDING THE BROKEN CIRCLE

Steve Heinrichs

This is the witness of
a Cree woman named Amanda,
gift of Creator,
herald of old memories,
the Word made fresh in Winnipeg,
a ceremony of change.

¤

Not long ago, a teenager came to Amanda. His name was Cody, and he had Fetal Alcohol Spectrum Disorder. Cody wept as he told her his story; how he was rejected and misunderstood by so many; how he didn't like himself and some of the things he did. Cody begged Amanda to heal him. Moved with compassion, Amanda hugged him, cried with him, and said, "Know that you are loved by Creator as you are, right now. You are broken, yes, but so very beautiful." And then she prayed. "Spirit, heal my brother." Instantly, Cody's brain was made whole. And his heart too.

Then Amanda sent him on his way with a warning, "Know that the world in which we currently live has judged you. It'll be terribly hard to shake that—if not impossible. People have decided to put their trust in authorities and experts, not in experience. So go to the specialists and get the doctors to examine you and confirm that you've been healed. They won't know what to make of this, but their word will get you a way back into the circle."

Amazed by his new-found healing, Cody not only told the doctors,

but everyone with ears to hear. As a result, Amanda couldn't go anywhere without a crowd showing up. To secure some alone time, she
tucked away to those forgotten places.

¤

When Amanda returned to the North End later that week, word
leaked out that she was back in town. Soon the house where she was
staying was jam-packed with visitors, so many that the front porch
was overflowing with those longing for a chance to see her. Amanda
was busy, passionately calling people to enact Creator's heart here and
now. "Can you hear the groans of creation? Industrial civilization is
dismantling us all, the Earth, our relatives, our souls. We've got to embrace God and her covenant, and you can't do that without embracing
one another and the land — this land."

While she was teaching, four men carried a quadriplegic to the
house. His name was Hank, and he wasn't born this way. He got hit by a
drunk driver when he was little. Since the house was so full, and it was
too hard to get people to make way, Hank's friends decided to dismantle a side bay window in order to get him in. Seeing the tremendous
lengths they were going to (and their obvious hope), Amanda looked at
Hank and said, "The compassion of Creator rests on you, my brother. I
know your situation. Your poor health has forced you to accumulate a
lot of debt, hasn't it? You owe the system, and the system owns you. But
I say to you, don't worry about that anymore. It's forgiven."

Taken aback by Amanda's words, a number of folks in the room
started grumbling amongst one another. "Where does she get off saying such things?" "Only the bank can release him from his debt." "All
this attention must be going to her head. Talking about Creator is fine,
but this is going too far!"

Amanda could read their faces and their hearts. She asked the
crowd, "What's most important to you? Money? Health? Right relations? But so that you know that the human who acts like a truly human one has authority to address all life —" she turned to Hank and
said, "Get up and go home! Enjoy your wife and children to the full-
est." And he did exactly that. Hank leaped to his feet, hugged Amanda,
and ran out of the house. Everyone was stunned.

Amazed, some joined hands, formed a circle, and offered prayers of thanksgiving.

¤

Amanda went down to Portage and Main, teaching the crowds that gathered round her. As she was speaking, she noticed out of the corner of her eye a young woman sitting on her briefcase, eating a hot dog, and listening attentively. Laurel was a HudBay Mining employee, an Ojibway from Sagkeeng First Nation. She was what some called an "Indian whisperer," one who tried to get Indigenous communities to open themselves up for resource extraction projects. In the middle of sentence, Amanda stopped speaking and walked right up to Laurel, and in front of the huge crowd said to her, "Follow me. I want you to join my circle." And immediately, Laurel left everything and followed.

Later that day, Laurel invited Amanda and her friends back to her place for dinner. Others joined them; fellow mining executives, some pipeline engineers and many others of disrepute. But there were some from the leftist-activist community who were disturbed by what they saw, and they asked Amanda's friends, "Why does she eat with the co-opted? They're all collaborators!" When Amanda got word, she intentionally confronted them, "You can sit in your circle of the converted and get little accomplished. Or you can work tirelessly to bring more into the fold. Yes, the under-resourced and oppressed (those who you talk a lot about, but I don't see you actually with) will always be with us. And yes, even folks like these, folks whose values have gone astray, yet sense that things aren't working, they are welcome too."

Night and day among the tombs and on the mountains he was always howling and bruising himself with stones. When he saw Jesus from a distance, he ran and bowed down before him.

Mark 5:5–6

BEYOND THE STRONG MAN

Ralph Armbruster-Sandoval

ON APRIL 4, 1967, one year before he was assassinated, Dr. Martin Luther King Jr. delivered his most radical and probably most overlooked speech, "A Time to Break Silence." Until that moment, King had said very little about the Vietnam War, but in this address, delivered at the historic Riverside Church in New York City, he declared that "silence was betrayal." While he spoke eloquently against the war on moral and ethical grounds, he also stated it was time to "go beyond Vietnam," asserting that the war was a "symptom of a far deeper malady within the American spirit." King correctly foresaw that, unless we addressed the root causes of the Vietnam War, people would be marching against ceaseless, never-ending conflicts around the world (think Iraq and Afghanistan). King thus went beyond opposition. He proposed something new — a "radical revolution in values," the only thing, he believed, that could save the United States from our "tragic death wish."

In the mid-1960s, President Johnson was the proverbial "strong man" from Mark's Gospel who so many people opposed. After him came more strong men — Nixon, Carter, Reagan, Bush Sr., Clinton, Bush Jr., and Obama. Now, dramatically and quite frighteningly, a new seemingly stronger man — Trump — has ascended to power, threatening nuclear war with North Korea and attacking immigrants, women, people of colour, queer people, and those with disabilities. And lest we forget, he has mocked climate change as nothing more than "fake news."

So Trump, one might reasonably argue, is today's strong man. And people from all over the world are asking themselves, "How do we bind or tie him down?" While understandable, what if this isn't the right question? We have seen strong men come and go, but what has endured is empire and its tentacles — racism, sexism, heterosexism, ecocide, ableism, and so much more. This is what King observed: it was time to move from opposing to proposing, it was time to not only break silence about the Vietnam War, but to call for a "radical revolution in values." In other words, if King were with us, I can imagine him telling us it's time to go "beyond Trump" and redirect our focus on "binding *him*."

Such rhetoric might seem fanciful, even absurd. But consider Jesus' strategy in Mark 5. Upon meeting the demoniac man, he asked him his name. The demoniac replied "Legion, for we are many." A legion was the largest division of Roman soldiers, containing some 5,000 men. The Romans were occupying Palestine and oppressing the Indigenous peoples for imperial gain. While the demoniac tells Jesus his name, what's most fascinating here is his explanation—"for we are many." The English poet Shelley wrote something similar nearly two centuries ago in *The Masque of Anarchy*, a political piece invoking non-violent resistance—"We are many and they are few."

Read that again. We are many. They are few.

Seen from this perspective, the demoniac might be telling Jesus a powerful and subversive truth — that the people constitute an army. Not a colonizing, imperial army, but a liberatory and de-colonizing force that can bind and tie down the strong man. The strong man is actually weak because the people are stronger—"we are many, they are few." The discourse parallels the language of the Occupy Movement—"we are the 99 percent!" That movement, which was short-lived and vilified as ineffective, did not focus on the "strong man," but targeted the broader socio-economic system called Wall Street (capitalism).

Tragically, we too often believe that the strong man cannot be challenged. In Mark's story, the strong man repeatedly breaks free and wreaks havoc. Each time this occurs, he's gagged, bound, and tortured. Upon seeing Jesus, he fears even more physical pain. But this is not Jesus' way. Jesus takes sides — he hears the cries of the poor (who are powerful and yet powerless) — and takes restorative action, healing the demoniac. Tellingly, the people's response is fear. They are frightened because they fear greater repression. So they keep their heads down, hoping that the once-possessed strong man will go away. They don't believe that they are "many," so they turn inward, forgetting who they are. They are not Legion; they are human beings struggling to be free, wanting to be treated with dignity and respect.

So there are two strong men in this story. The demoniac represents the Roman Empire and Trump. They are strong and powerful. But the people are stronger and can not only bind the strong man, they can also push for a whole new way of life. Jesus wasn't only concerned with binding the Powers That Be. He, like King, called for a "radical revolution in values." He worked to create a world where the "first shall be last and the last shall be first" (Mark 10:31).

Trump is strong but he's a symptom of a "far deeper malady," as King would say. It is time to "go beyond Trump," to suggest what we are for rather than what we are against. It is time to remember who we are. "We are many"—strong, resilient, compassionate, and loving. Together we can drive out the demon and the system he upholds. In this "long and bitter but beautiful struggle for a new world," as King said, we must keep our "eyes on the prize." Being anti-Trump or anti-capitalist or anti-war isn't sufficient. One must turn the world upside down, recognizing just how powerful we are.

He has brought down the
powerful from their thrones,
and lifted up the lowly;
he has filled the hungry with
good things, and sent the rich
away empty.

Luke 1:52–53

AN URGENT LETTER

Kwok Pui-lan

DEAR ELIZABETH,

You may be surprised that I am writing you, since I don't have much education and don't often write. But I am so distraught and must ask your advice, for you are much older and wiser than me.

Yesterday when I visited my neighbour Rivka, she whispered into my ear that she had heard rumours about me. Several women had said that I was so naïve that I had been cheated and taken advantage of. Though they thought me innocent, they said I had brought shame to my family.

This is the furthest thing from the truth. I've always been a strong woman who can make up my own mind. And you have been my role model! I've learned so much from you, Elizabeth. When I was small, you told me stories about Sarah, Miriam, and the prophetess Deborah. I admired their courage and their leadership qualities. I especially admired Miriam, who helped her brothers Aaron and Moses deliver the Jewish people from bondage. Just like them, I want to lead a useful life. I want to contribute to my family and our people.

When the angel visited me and told me that I would bear a son, I was surprised and asked, humbly, "How will this be, since I am a virgin?" Yet I knew that a woman is not defined by her biology, and that one could be a mother outside marriage. You might think that I was too daring when I conceded to this, but I knew that God had a plan for me. I didn't mind stepping outside of society's gender norms. I didn't mind being labelled an "unwed mother." I have seen how people look down upon those mothers and stigmatize their children, labelling them "illegitimate." It's totally unfair. We require women and young girls to be pure and chaste, but we never require the same from men.

Elizabeth, I know that you too have not been content with how society treats women. You've always been a faithful and righteous woman. But your family—and especially your in-laws—disrespected you before you bore a child. Although you took such good care of Zechariah's house and helped him in the temple whenever you could, they didn't give you credit for doing so. Instead, they gossiped behind your back and teased you.

Yet you are a strong woman, Elizabeth. And you don't believe that biology is destiny. You have wondered all your life why a woman's worth is defined by her ability to give birth to children. I have seen you offer solace to Auntie Chava when her daughter could not conceive. And I knew that you brought food and ointment to your neighbour when her daughter-in-law miscarried. You have been such a good example to me!

You were the first one I wanted to talk to after the angel visited, for I needed your advice. I still remember that you were almost six months pregnant and your baby bump was showing. I wanted to know what it was like being pregnant, since I'm young and have no experience. You were so glad to see me—even the baby leaped in your womb when I greeted you. You told me not to be afraid, and blessed me, and said that our children would grow up healthy and resilient and become leaders of our people. Your blessings really gave me strength, and I knew that I would be alright. And then you allowed me to stay with you during my first months of pregnancy, taking such tender care of me. I wish other women would have such generous support from their female relatives and friends when they endure trying times!

When I saw the way that people mistreated you when you were barren—as they do so many other allegedly "unchaste" women—my heart sank. There's been so much injustice inflicted upon women. Our lives are too hard. In my village, the widow Esther became so poor that she had to sell her body at the village gate, and Baruch's wife has become ill from anxiety about how to feed her family (you might have heard that Baruch's legs were broken when his fishing boat capsized in the stormy winds last summer).

It's obvious to all of us. The rich who live in the cities of Jerusalem and Jericho don't really care about the oppressed in the countryside. Poor Ariel had to sell a portion of his land because he couldn't afford to pay the heavy taxes. It's unbelievable, all these taxes that we have to pay—imperial taxes, local taxes, and temple taxes—and the amount keeps increasing each year! And the tax collector always collects extra to fatten his pockets! My father is deeply concerned about his vineyard. He wonders how long we might be able to keep the land Grandpa has passed onto us.

Life under empire is wearying. I dream of the day that God will deliver us from the Romans. As God protected our ancestors from the Egyptians and the Babylonians, God is able to deliver us from foreign rule now. We would no longer need to pay such brutal taxes. We wouldn't need to be submissive and compliant when the tax-collectors and imperial officials come around. We could have our own small portion of land, grow some olive trees, bake bread for our children and grandchildren, and watch them grow. I long for this simple life. It's not too much to ask, is it?

But now there are rumours about me, which make me terribly sad. Elizabeth, you know my story from the beginning. What should I do now? Very soon people will be able to see that I am pregnant, and they'll all know. How can I explain that to Joseph's family? I need your advice, Elizabeth, please help me.

With love,
Mary

Then the devil led him up and showed him in an instant all the kingdoms of the world. And the devil said to him, "To you I will give their glory and all this authority; for it has been given over to me, and I give it to anyone I please."

Luke 4:5–6

RECLAIMING PEOPLE POWER

Joerg Rieger

IMAGINE BEING OFFERED power and authority over a good chunk of the world. Now imagine that offer packaged with other sweet promises, such as unlimited abundance and protection. How tempting would that be?

The level of enticement, I assume, depends largely on who is being tempted. In classical colonial situations, like the ones we have experienced in the Americas, the colonizers would have been so sure of themselves that the promise of power and authority would have been enough for them to cut a deal with the devil. Today, the world of big trade and big business—where profit eclipses people and the very earth itself—continues the colonial way with zeal and reckless abandon.

Others are less interested in domination—they just want to help. For them, the promise of power and authority, and the benefits of abundance and protection, are less self-serving. Think of well-intentioned men and women who enter the arenas of government and state bureaucracy. Some are prepared to make a deal with the devil—to "set aside those illusions of purity," "to get one's hands dirty"—if it means they can attain positions of control from which they can help more people. The trade-off is not only sensible, but seemingly required. One can see it as a sacrifice "for the greater good."

But not Jesus. He emphatically rejects such top-down power and authority, as well as the abundance and protection it supposedly guarantees. And it appears that his rejection is permanent. Bear in mind that if the wilderness-tested-Jesus was expecting that God would eventually give him all that the devil promised just a short while later, these temptations would not have amounted to much. Something else is going on. Jesus has no interest in the top-down power model, represented in his time by the colonizing Roman Empire and its allies in Galilee and Judea. He's against it. Even if it's used to help people.

Some have concluded from the story of Jesus' temptation that power, abundance, and protection are to be rejected altogether. Chastened colonizers as well as frustrated helpers might well come to this determination. Yet as the colonized and those struggling to make ends meet know full well, this is hardly an option.

If we follow the story of Jesus through to the end of Luke's gospel, we come across a hopeful idea. While Jesus rejects the top-down power of the colonizers and the one percent, he models a different sort of power. His is rooted in people, who he encourages and animates through preaching, teaching, and organizing. And thus we see Jesus, not only refusing the abundance of the ruling class, but modelling a particular way of realizing abundance through non-possessive sharing of money and material goods so that all are fed. And we see Jesus rejecting the protection and security offered by top-down power through wealth and military force, yet modelling another kind of protection through his efforts to form communities of radical care and solidarity.

When Jesus stands up to the temptations of hegemonic power and the abundance and protection that it offers, he is clearly taking the side of the disinherited, the exploited, the oppressed, the working poor, the blessed down-and-out. In so doing, he reclaims the power of the people that works from the bottom up.

Jesus-inspired movements throughout history show that this is not just a pious dream. In the Americas, it was people's movements that ended slavery, child labour, and many other forms of discrimination; and it was people's movements that achieved universal suffrage, labour laws, social security regulations, and many other benefits. Much remains to be done, to be sure, but we now know where to look for hope.

And he rolled up the scroll, gave it back to the attendant, and sat down. The eyes of all in the synagogue were fixed on him. Then he began to say to them, "Today this scripture has been fulfilled in your hearing."

Luke 4:20–21

GO LISTEN

Rachel and Chris Brnjas

Moving to a season of hope,
anticipating new life,
we consider matters of faith, land, and justice
as we ponder the world a little one might enter.
In this light, we write:

To our unborn child,

You were born into a beautiful
and messy world.

We are your parents, and we deeply love you.
We are sorry that the world we brought you into is so messy,
that it divides black and white,
good and bad,
conservative and liberal.
This is not the way that Creator made the world.

We are Christian.
We follow and love Jesus.

It is our gift for you
and you can choose to do with it whatever
your heart tells you.
But Christians have carried a curse into this land.

Some would pretend that God favours us
because we are Christian, because we are
"good"
"a chosen people"
"the Lord's anointed."

We Christians went to the ends of the world
and shared our "good news."
Many believe that we did what
we were supposed to do:
We saw the "unenlightened,"
those with different cultures and traditions—
and we tried to make them like us.
We thought our voices, our stories
were the only ones. The sacred ones.

We were so quick to spread our gospel,
that we forgot to listen
to the wisdom in the cultures we "discovered."
Jesus was good at listening.
We shut ears and hearts
to the sacred ones as we
built up a large country
in our own image.

Child, when we forget to listen,
we forget who we are.

We pray for you,
as we pray for ourselves.
May your heart be moved to pursue
the well-being of others—
the prisoners, the blind, and the oppressed.
May you see their beauty and their light,
and may they see yours.

It is time to listen.

Be brave, child.
Listen to your heart.
Listen to the voices of those overlooked.
Listen to the land.
Listen to the Spirit's movement.

You were born into a beautiful world.
Messy, but beautiful.
Go listen
and receive light.
Go listen
and share your light too.

And the Word became flesh and lived among us, and we have seen his glory, the glory as of a father's only son, full of grace and truth.

John 1:14

FOR GOD SO LOVED

Rebecca Voelkel

In the beginning were Desire and Longing:
  Desire for ecstasy and connection, longing for the deepest of
  communions.

And Desire and Longing were with God.
  And Desire and Longing were God.
    Desire and Longing were with God in the beginning.

In fact, they were the animators, the prodders, the relentless whispers
  which propelled the explosion of creativity:
    stars and planets and the whole company of creation. These all came
      into being out
        of that Desire and Longing, and not one thing would have been
          without
            the promise of ecstasy, connection, and communion.

And then, as now, Desire and Longing were threatening to the forces of
  destruction, dis-connection, dismemberment, and death.

But then, as now, these did not prevail and what came into being
because of and through
  Desire and Longing
    were
      Life, and Life abundant.

¤

It was early September 2017 in the Upper Midwest of the United States. It was on Dakota land that had been stolen by Settlers over 200 years ago. It was in front of a predominantly white, suburban congregation which had engaged in study around the Doctrine of Discovery— Church law that baptized genocide, chattel slavery, and the wholesale theft of land; Church law that had been codified into U.S. law.

It was in that time and that place that the lone protestor held a sign: "Homo sex is sin." The white, Settler, presumably-straight and presumably-cisgender man wanted to intimidate the congregation, it seemed, as they entered their sanctuary for worship. His presence, with his anger, judgment, and threatened violence, was an embodiment of the ways in which his Christian ancestors had literally thrown the two-spirit/ gender non-conforming/gay "savages" to the dogs when they first encountered First Nations peoples in this hemisphere. His presence was an embodiment of the connection between the permission to commit genocide against Indigenous peoples and the permission to destroy perceived sexual perversion. His presence was a reminder that the forces of dis-connection, dismemberment, and destruction don't discriminate.

As they walked into the sanctuary, several congregants talked amongst themselves about what to do. They had voted long ago to be welcoming and affirming of queer, lesbian, bisexual, gay, and transgender people. And they had lived up to their promises over the years. So they wondered how to engage this man and his sign. They made the explicit connection between the colonizing violence of Indigenous genocide and the colonizing violence of homo-hating. But how might they witness to the Word/Desire/Longing become Flesh?

One teenager whose gender identity was still in process said to the pastor, "I want to go talk with him."

As they walked toward him, they breathed in:

In the beginning were Desire and Longing, connection and communion.

Before they got all the way to where the protestor stood, they paused and said, "We just want you to know that we love you."

His face did not change, his sign did not come down. He still glared and menaced.

But in that moment, Desire and Longing, connection and communion, became flesh. That teenage, genderqueer person, was a witness and a testimony to the promise of life, and life abundant. They were not life themselves, but they pointed toward life. And their actions, their impulse, pointed toward true communion.

¤

That true communion, that ecstasy and connection which enlivens everyone, is coming into the world. S/he was in the world, and the world came into being through them; yet the world did not know them. S/he came to what was their own, but their own people did not accept them. But to all who received them, who believed in their name, s/he gave the power to become the children of God, who were born, not of the forces of destruction and hatred, not of the impulse to harm, but of God.

And the Word/Desire/Longing became flesh and lived among us, and we have seen their radiance and we have felt their invitation, their sacred pull and tug toward God, their sometimes-inexplicable impulse toward one another. In this Incarnation, in this embodiment of Word/Desire/Longing, we have seen and felt this one who is Beloved of the Creator, like a child precious to a parent. (And the one who had come before them but was not them, testified and cried out, "This was s/he of whom I said, 'S/he who was born after me but is a fuller expression of the Divine because they were present at the beginning.'")

From this Incarnate One we have all received passion upon passion, connection upon connection, blessing and grace upon blessing and grace. The law indeed was given through Moses; passion, connection, blessing, grace, and the truth of communion came through Jesus the Christ, the Incarnate One. No one has ever seen God/Creator. It is God the precious child, born of God's longing and desire, who is close to Creator's heart, who has made Longing/Desire/God known to us.

A Samaritan woman came to draw water, and Jesus said to her, "Give me a drink."

John 4:7

STOLEN WATERS, THIRSTY PEOPLE

Susanne Guenther Loewen

HE COULD'VE GONE to any of the 85 Indigenous communities in Canada that are currently under boil-water advisories. But he chose to go to Shoal Lake 40 First Nation, or Kekekoziibii, Hawk River. This is the one that supplies the city of Winnipeg with water; the one where the city's aquifer cuts the community off from the mainland; the one that gives drink to three-quarters of a million people, but whose own people go thirsty.

So he took the small, slow barge from the mainland and arrived on the shore of the artificial island. Tired from his journey, he sat down by the community hall. It was about noon.

A woman came to haul her water, the blue plastic jugs a heavy burden. And he said to her, "Could I have a drink?" (His friends had gone to Kenora to buy food.)

She said to him, "How is it that you, an outsider, ask a drink of me, a member of this community?" (No one usually came to Shoal Lake 40 to drink the water.) "I should be asking you for a drink of water!" she joked.

"If you asked me," he said, "I would give you living water."

The woman said to him, "But you have no water jug. You have nothing to boil water in. Where would you get that living water?"

He said to her, "You're right. Today, everyone who drinks of this water will be thirsty again, but those who drink of their own, living water will never be thirsty. One day soon, living water will become in you a spring of pure, clean water, gushing up to sustain your children forever."

The woman said to him, "I hope so. We've been longing and working for this water so that we may never be thirsty or have to keep coming here to haul water."

He said to her, "Go, call your husband and come back."

She answered, "I have no husband."

He said to her, "You're right in saying that you have no husband. You lost him last winter when he fell through the ice, trying to cross to the mainland. This community has suffered too many years of broken promises, ever since that aquifer was built 100 years ago from the disturbed bones of your ancestors."

The woman looked at him for a while. Then she said to him, "I see you know about our history. We've been passed back and forth between levels of government for decades. No one wants to take responsibility for honouring the treaties. Our people say that this land and water are sacred, that this is where we meet Creator. But for the Settlers, land and water are just resources to be bought and sold; that's what's sacred to them."

He said to her, "Believe me, the hour is coming when the treaties will be honoured, when Settlers and Indigenous peoples will bless each other, when the spirit of true reconciliation will no longer be a far-off dream, but will dwell among us. The hour is coming, and is now here, when Jews and Christians will remember what their sacred Scriptures say: 'let justice roll down like waters, and righteousness like an ever-flowing stream'" (Amos 5:24).

The woman said to him, "I know that our Freedom Road is coming, and once it's built, we'll no longer be cut off. We'll be able to clean our water and quench our thirst again."

Jesus said to her, "I know what it's like to be thirsty. I'm the one who once said, 'Blessed are those who hunger and thirst for righteousness, for they will be filled' (Matthew 5:6). And I'm with you as you continue to work for justice, for the living water that will sustain your children and grandchildren forever."

He entered his headquarters again and asked Jesus, "Where are you from?" But Jesus gave him no answer. Pilate therefore said to him, "Do you refuse to speak to me? Do you not know that I have power to release you, and power to crucify you?"

John 19:9–10

UNHOLY ALLIANCES

Joshua Grace

"Crucify him!"

We can scarcely imagine crowds shouting such words today. Yet similar sentiment gets expressed in subtle ways. I've been attending Delaware River Basin Commission hearings on fracking proposals for a decade, as well as Energy Hub project meetings, and our hard-won moratorium on drilling has been challenged this year. The gas industry could stir the crowds with rousing chants—"Let's create more jobs!" "We want cheap energy!" But it need not. Most Americans are already there. It could stir the crowds against Host peoples (the genuine title holders) as it did in the past—"Kill the Lenape!" "Get rid of their ways!" But it need not. Settler society has long ignored the jurisdiction of Original peoples. They are nothing but invisible barriers to promised-land wealth that will be overcome for the industry's vision of the common good.

"I find no case against him!"

The history of the Lenni-Lenape in this watershed—a place I've lived for some 20 years—goes back a remarkable 10 millennia. Lenapehoking (land of the Lenape) has been sustained since time immemorial by the Lenapewhittuck (rapid stream of the Lenape people). Now called the Delaware, the river and her watershed currently act as home to 15 million people. She begins in the Catskill Mountains of New York State and includes 216 tributaries, giving life to parts of Pennsylvania, Delaware,

Maryland, and New Jersey before becoming part of the Atlantic Ocean. Three major bands of Lenape spread across this large region, forming towns around agriculture and hunting.

For most of us, what little Lenape history we know comes through the eyes and records of Settlers. We are told that Dutch traders brought smallpox and other new diseases to Lenapehoking beginning in the early 1600s. Over the next 50 years, neighbouring groups like the Iroquois would lose as much as half their population to the disease. Lenape losses are unclear. Yet we do know that by the late 17th century, the Lenape were still the majority population in the region spanning from Delaware to Southern New York, across to Eastern Pennsylvania. Despite Settler claims about "the vanishing Indian," the Lenape did not go away. And they're still here, living, present, and standing before today's crowds who dismiss all claims of Native sovereignty in their hunger for Lenape resources.

"We have a law!"

The extraction industry intentionally misinforms the watching world about the ecological damage their projects will inflict in order to forge an unholy alliance between the people and the powers of profit. The government of the United States quietly maintains their "legal" system of settler colonial dispossession—founded upon the Christian Doctrine of Discovery—to assimilate and suppress the blood-cries of the land. And as most of us capitulate ourselves to short-term benefits, we inflict apocalyptic aggression on the earth and her Original peoples to the benefit of the rich.

But some, like Jesus before Pilate, hold on to a strange hope: That from the depths of the tragic, an unimaginable possibility might rise.

"Where are you from?"

It's possible that the most renowned of Lenape chiefs, Tamanend, treatied with the Quaker William Penn—founder of "the Holy Experiment" and the Commonwealth of Pennsylvania—in my neighbourhood, back in 1683. His prophecy, that the Lenape and English would "live in peace as long as the waters run in the rivers and creeks, and as long as the stars and moon endure," was trampled on by the next generation of Settlers. Penn's sons, Thomas and John, destroyed the original document that put the Holy Experiment into motion. They then tarnished their father's reputation through a fraudulent land grab known as the Walking Purchase; more than a million acres of Lenape territory were claimed, and the Lenape were forced to vacate.

During the French and Indian War of 1754–63, the Lenape, like so many Indigenous nations, were caught between imperial desires. At times, the Lenape fought with the French against the British. At other times, when power dynamics shifted, they fought with the British — whatever they could do to hold on to some of their territory, let alone safeguard the survival of their community.

In 1758, the Lenape signed the Treaty of Easton with the British, and in the process, ceded all their claims to the territory within the Province of New Jersey. When the United States declared their independence from the British in 1776, some Lenape were forced to relocate to southern Ontario. In 1778, the United States then signed its first Treaty at Fort Pitt, present-day Pittsburgh. This sacred covenant gave the U.S. permission to travel throughout Lenape territory. But it also, quite remarkably, recognized the Lenape as sovereign and encouraged the formation of a pan-Indigenous state "whereof the Delaware nation [Lenape] shall be the head, and have a representation in Congress." Unsurprisingly, the Treaty fell apart a year later. Most believe the U.S. had no intentions of ever recognizing Lenape sovereignty.

Put on trial, with colonial judge and jury, the powers ask the Lenape, "Where are you from?" And just as Pilate's parameters for Jesus' sense of place were too restricted, the Settler authorities can't comprehend the Lenape's connection to "the lands, territories, and resources which they have traditionally owned, occupied, or otherwise used or acquired" (Article 27, *United Nations Declaration on the Rights of Indigenous Peoples*).

Jesus gave him no answer.

The United States recognizes three Delaware Tribes; two in Oklahoma and one in Wisconsin. Canada recognizes three Lenape First Nations who have four reserves in Southwestern Ontario. Smaller groups not recognized by states or the federal government reside in Maryland, Idaho, Delaware, Kansas, Pennsylvania, Oklahoma, Ohio, and New Jersey.

As connections to traditional territories are stretched, connections to the languages of the land are also threatened. The Lenape language is presently in danger of being lost to all but a handful of scholars. Some are resisting that loss, evidenced in the Lenape Language Preservation Project in Oklahoma, which is attempting to revive the Unami dialect. There's also a group in Ontario that is speaking Munsee. But the powers of colonialism weigh heavy.

Jesus was silent before Pilate. Did he lose his voice? Did he surrender it? Did he respond to the colonial violence by speaking another hidden language? The language of his life, his way? The Lenape voice has been under constant colonial surveillance and silencing. They understand Jesus' experience. And his response.

"We have no king but Caesar!"

By the 1770s, many colonists considered Chief Tamanend (called "Tammany") the patron saint of America. Some used him to prop their political aspirations, making an oppositional claim to the British Crown that they "had no king but Tammany." Secret political societies formed along the East coast, the most famous in New York's Tammany Hall. Until 1776 and the Declaration of Independence, Philadelphia rang all the church bells on May 1 to remember Tamanend, the Affable One.

Settler exploitation of Tamanend in support of nativist ideologies shows just how far a story can be skewed to bless the ways of Caesar. It reminds me of the bust of Chief Tamanend that was made for the USS Delaware. After the Civil War, the bust was patched up and placed outside the U.S. Naval Academy in Annapolis, Maryland. But the sailors didn't like what Tamanend represented. He was a pacifist. So they re-named the statue Tecumseh after the Shawnee warrior (and ally of the British). That's how settler colonial society works. It forges alliances when it's convenient to their cause — even if it blasphemes relationships with people, the land, and truth itself. For as Pilate opined, "What is truth?"

Yet despite the many public betrayals, relocations, confinements, as-similations, and lies, the Lenape endure. They rise up, continually, even in dance, offering to share with the next generation the incredible gifts of their worldview, culture, practice, and language. And so does this bruised and battered Lenape land and watershed. Despite repeated torture and public execution, this place that I call home defies the colonial state's dream of transforming Philadelphia into an Energy Hub. As with Jesus, we may wonder about the future of the Lenape and Lenapehoking. But the crowds who want death are in for a surprise.

And suddenly from heaven there came a sound like the rush of a violent wind, and it filled the entire house where they were sitting.

Acts 2:2

VOICES RISE

Joy De Vito

A rush of wind scatters the strategic plans
and negotiators scramble to escape.
They breathe a sigh of relief as the flames pass by.

Then voices rise in a surge that
threatens the future of the
godly church-nation:

Mohawk
Oneida
Onondaga
Cayuga
Seneca
Tuscarora

Treaties, proclamations, deeds,
taken as opportunities to contain
Six Nations
in one pleasing package called
"Indigenous Peoples."

Yet documents are not enough
to restrain the sound.

The fearful dismiss the prophets as disruptors
of the peace or fools.
But ultimately, the easiest way forward
is to suggest a bottle in their hand
and assume that new language is the same
as the smell of booze on breath.

But what if some in the room heard a gift?

There would be no hierarchy of holiness,
no assigned seating,
as the growing chorus of voices
sought one another out.

Wampum remembered and treasured
might not bring ease
but could invite open comfort with the truth,
  measured by relationships
    not land.

Yet the spirit-infused sound was interrupted.

Tongues were silenced.

And nations were inexorably cornered
into one small portion of the promised land.

The alternative seems straightforward when
cultural festivals on stolen ground offer
an illusion of community life.
But shared food, resources, care, and sorrow
are only experienced
when the voices are first heard.

  Mohawk
  Oneida
  Onondaga

Cayuga
Seneca
Tuscarora

Listen.

Let every person be subject to the governing authorities; for there is no authority except from God, and those authorities that exist have been instituted by God. Therefore whoever resists authority resists what God has appointed, and those who resist will incur judgment.

Romans 13:1–2

RESISTANCE WITH LOVE

Daniel L. Smith-Christopher

IF YOU ARE going to live peacefully with all, then you also need to learn to overcome evil with good, and not use violence against violence. That never works.

That brings us to the issue of occupying soldiers; those who have declared themselves the "governing authorities." When it comes to the colonial forces, for heaven's sake, keep your heads down! If there is any order at all in this world, then it is because God is working to keep the world in one piece. Let the Romans flatter themselves into thinking this is because of their power and their presence. But they themselves are not more powerful than God.

As I said, keep your Jesus-loving heads down! Despite what his propaganda claims, Caesar has never been a man of peace—there is a reason all the occupying Roman soldiers have swords! If we make trouble for them, we will attract their attention, and nothing good ever comes from attracting Roman attention. And you know they will make it look like any trouble is our fault. So if you want to be unafraid of the Romans (and we are all tempted to fear them), then don't give them any excuse to make trouble for us. That is why we pay our taxes. After all, withholding our pitiful few coins is hardly going to make them pack up and march home. Just pay them and get on with it. Let them believe that they are important and that we somehow "owe" them something. Smile, give them their precious Roman coins, tell them, "What a nice shine you have on your helmet today, sir," and be happy when they grunt, "move on!" Let them go right on thinking they are so important. We know better. The only thing we truly "owe" anyone else is our love.

In fact, we shouldn't ever be led to believe that we "owe" anything to anyone — much less the Romans colonizers for their occupation and plunder. What we owe is love — as our Master showed us — even to those soldiers. After all, our brother Luke reminds us of the time that one of them felt guilty and unworthy because he was a powerful soldier here, in our land. And he actually humbled himself to call on Christ for help!

I know. I could hardly believe the story myself when I first heard it. A Roman?! I told him, "If you ever write up all these stories you have gathered about Jesus, don't leave out that one!"

As our Risen Teacher told us, this much we have learned. All of the lessons Moses taught us about not killing, not being jealous of other people's possessions, not interfering in other people's families and such, it all boils down to one basic, central idea: "Love others as much as you love yourself." And since loving others means doing nothing wrong to them, then love pretty much sums it all up. This kind of love takes all our attention, which is why we hardly need to worry about the self-deluding Romans (who, after all, love nobody else like they love themselves). "Governing authorities" indeed! We need to respect those to whom respect is due, and that's rarely them. Love is what is due to others, and it's hard work.

It is far into the day now. Evening approaches before that glorious new morning. We haven't got time to worry about the colonizer's delusions of grandeur. Their weapons are only darkness. But we have set aside all weapons of darkness and put on the defensive armour of light. So let's not waste time! And for goodness sake, let's not ourselves be tempted to act like the Romans, obsessed as they are with drink, sex, and constant fighting. For this they want honour and respect? We need not be afraid, for as I said, we've put on an armour of light. In a sense, we have "put on" Jesus Christ Himself as our armour. In the short time left, it would be ridiculous to reduce ourselves to Roman obsessions with merely self-indulged physical pleasures. Love for others is so much more than petty self-gratification. It is clear, isn't it? The way of Jesus couldn't be more different than the way of the Empire.

For it is written, "I will destroy the wisdom of the wise, and the discernment of the discerning I will thwart." Where is the one who is wise? Where is the scribe? Where is the debater of this age? Has not God made foolish the wisdom of the world?

1 Corinthians 1:19–20

NO GODS

David Driedger

GO AHEAD AND fool yourself, but I'll take my chances where I can get them. I don't know why you are reading this or what message you think you will get out of it. Anyway, forget about the "why." It's a dead end. I don't know you. I don't know if you are perishing or empowered, but I do know this: Life as we know it has demolished anything we might have considered sane.

Think I'm wrong? Think I'm fooling myself? Then tell me. Where is the person in power who genuinely acts in the interests of life and well-being? Don't trot out A-list activists or left-wing academics. The world has produced them, packaged them, and shipped them. Just another product for another market. No. I want you to show me the powerful men. The men of wealth and the men of violence. Then men of both. Show me where there is power and sanity. Show me the one, any one, concerned about rising sea levels and the endless nihilism of economic growth. The world has betrayed the earth and accommodated them all.

There is nothing left for the powerless to do in this world, so do what you want. Spend all your money on parties and feasts. Scrimp and save to feed the hungry. I don't care. Either way, it's foolishness in the face of the world. Line up next week's casualities. Is it a mass shooting? Garment factory collapse? Another hurricane? Military invasion? A run on anxiety and depression? You name it. Line them up, and they'll be mowed down by the wisdom of the world. Go on — show me a wisdom that will get us out of this.

I ask just one thing of you. Consider two words.

No gods.

Let it be a refrain.

No gods.

You thought we had left the gods to the past, as a quaint and primitive notion, but they surround us. What gathers attention (idols and advertising), what demands devotion (sovereign nations and slave labour), what determines value (money, money, money)? Answer: god. The gods have always ruled the world, and still do. So say it with me.

No gods.

Tell me of your god in the face of the earth's betrayal? There are none living worthily our faith. They are either killed or corrupted.

No gods.

If there is a wisdom to be had it will only come as that phrase permeates and reverberates, sounds and resounds. It can serve as a thin shield, or a hidden space. What else do you think will help? Degrees, status, or wealth? How's that working out for us? No. It is much more simple.

No gods.

Say it. You want a little comfort and healing and connection. Say it.

No gods.

Listen. Do you hear it?

No gods.

Go now. Gather there.

For all who rely on the works of the law are under a curse; for it is written, "Cursed is everyone who does not observe and obey all the things written in the book of the law."

Galatians 3:10

WHITE LAW

Alain Epp Weaver

THE LAW IS a curse in my neighbourhood of Lancaster, Pennsylvania. On morning and evening walks in Reservoir Park, I pass by the fortress-like county prison, with its twin castle towers, two blocks from my home. Opened in 1851, the Lancaster County Prison adopted the "penitentiary" architecture of prisons pioneered at Philadelphia's Eastern Penitentiary, a style inspired by a high-minded vision of reforming souls through reflective penitence.

Like other projects of aspiring modernity, the idealist visions driving the penitentiary model of incarceration have proven illusory. Until 1912, the prison served as the site of public hangings. Today, the prison is severely overcrowded, and conditions are grim: in 2015, three inmates hanged themselves. Like other prisons in the United States, the Lancaster County Prison contains a disproportionate number of people of colour, especially African Americans and individuals of Latin American heritage, thanks to pointed racial disparities in charging and sentencing. Forty-four percent of the prison's inmates come from communities of colour, even though persons of colour only make up 15 percent of the county's total population.

When the law of the land is the white supremacist rule of mass incarceration, the law is a curse. But even though I know how twisted and hell-bent this law is, I recognize that the damned thing has a hold on me. I'm foolishly bewitched by it.

As I take my daily walks through the verdant public park next to my house, I'm all-too-easily seduced by the vision of myself as a good, law-abiding citizen, who has attained material comforts and social status thanks to my merits and hard work. I'm entranced by the allure of set-ting up a divide in my mind and soul, a divide between myself — some-one who follows and respects the rules — and all those law-breakers in-side the prison. I'm tempted to turn away from and not recognize the many and various ways I benefit as a white man who lives within the rules and regulations shaped by the underlying law of white supremacy in the United States. I delude myself into thinking that the benefits I accrue from this oppressive system count as righteousness for me. And in doing so, I not only develop an idolatrous self-understanding, but I endanger the relationship that I really do have with my incarcerat-ed brothers and sisters, a relationship created and sustained by the One who made us all.

The apostle Paul was unequivocal. Our righteousness comes not through our own efforts or making, our own faithfulness or law-keep-ing. It comes solely through faith in the righteousness of God, the gra-cious gift of the Spirit. This is the faith modelled by Abraham and Sarah, who put their trust in God alone as they set out to a new land. This is the faith of Hagar, who cried out in the wilderness to God after being sent out from Abraham and Sarah's tent. This is the faith of the Galilean carpenter who was publicly executed for proclaiming freedom for the captives, the one who preached the dawning reign of love and justice as an alternative to the law of brutal occupation. This is the faith of those in the Lancaster prison and across the United States who are pressed but not crushed by a racist justice system.

It is so easy for those who have privilege to be bewitched by the law. And I imagine that it's easy for those locked up by this power to slip into despair. Lord have mercy. Strengthen the faith of those who resist the destructive law of white supremacy. Clear the minds of us who are possessed by it. And move us to right-setting relationship.

And being found in human form, he humbled himself and became obedient to the point of death—even death on a cross.

Philippians 2:7–8

DANCING WITH GOD

Anita L. Keith

The people needed a Saviour
Someone to call their own
The enemy had come, killed, destroyed
The ones they had loved and known
Devastation lay all around
Could He hear from on high, from above?

A Lamb was provided
He was chosen, he was the one
He walked humbly and obediently
He submitted to what had to be
They pierced his flesh till it bled and fastened him to the tree
Then pulled Him up high for everyone one to see

All day he hung in the merciless sun's heat
The night came, there was no relief
He was committed to the journey, to the atonement for sin
He gladly and willingly paid the price
He was, after all, the living sacrifice

The teachings of the Elders came back to him like a flood
The Sun Dance was the way a young brave showed his love
He knew it was time, time to step up
To the tree, his life he would give
In hopes that his loved ones would be blessed and live

The young brave remembered the dance
A dance between Creator and him
A dance of the soul touching God
And in that moment the heavens opened anew
He made petitions for others, for the many, for the few
It was an interchange between Spirit and Spirit
A giving of himself; a time to let go
A humbling of oneself and trusting heaven's flow

The four days had come and gone
Carefully and slowly they lowered Him down
The brave weathered His journey well
Weakened he stopped and centred himself on the ground

Then with one last surge of energy he pushed backwards as
    hard as he could
He felt the bone trusses rip at his body, they ripped at his chest
Weary from his journey, he prayed for rest
He had laboured hard, his strength was now diminished
Then gently and softly he whispered, "It is finished."

¤

I am a Mohawk woman living in Plains territory. For generations, the Sun Dance—an integral ceremony to the Blackfoot, Cheyenne, Cree, Dakota, Lakota, and Nakoda—was practised routinely in these lands. Once criminalized by colonial powers (until 1934 in the United States; 1951 in Canada), the Sun Dance is currently experiencing a resurgence, as young and older rediscover traditional lifeways.

I am a Christian woman. And my question is whether the Church can see Jesus, the cruciform servant, in the warrior of the Sun Dance? Can we celebrate this centuries-old ritual that sustains Indigenous communities? Or is that beyond our imagining? Is it pagan?

I see the Spirit at work in the Sun Dancer. Does he utter the name of Jesus? No. But the more profound question is: Does he behave like Jesus? Now this is where we begin to feel discomfort.

The seed of God is planted in every heart. At birth we are acutely aware of someone greater than ourselves, someone who made us. When I look at the Sun Dancer, I perceive the heart of that One. In Philippians 2, Paul calls us to have the same mind as Christ, the same love, and to be of one accord. That quality is evident in the young warrior. He goes to the tree in humbleness of mind, not valuing himself better than others, but considering the needs of the wider circle. The warrior makes himself a servant and becomes obedient unto pain, and if need be, death. He allows Creator to work in him and through him to gift others. And it is Creator's good pleasure that he Sun Dance, offering prayer for the well-being of the people.

What of us? When the Spirit calls us to sacrifice for others, will we submit, give, and go?

If with Christ you died to the elemental spirits of the universe, why do you live as if you still belonged to the world? Why do you submit to regulations, "Do not handle, do not taste, do not touch"? All these regulations refer to things that perish with use; they are simply human commands and teachings.

Colossians 2:20—22

GOOD NEWS TO THE COLONIZED?

Neil Elliott

LET ME MAKE this simple so you can understand it. The god Christ wants you to give up life in your body: the way you dress your hair, the signs in and on your skin, how your people have marked you as one of them, and how you have learned to mark yourself as yourself; the turns, glides, and stops of your people's speech, the ways you speak with your eyes to one another; all the ways you have learned to present yourself among your people. All that is dead: worse, shameful. But the god Christ delivers you from the shame of being one of them.

The god Christ has done away with your past, as if burned in a fire. The ways of your people, your customs, your stories, the prohibitions that safeguard your community, the myths that warm and gladden your hearts when you gather to retell them, the rhythms of your drums and flutes, your songs and dances: all that was filth and death. The god Christ has delivered you from yourself, from the false honour and joy you thought you carried as you went in and out among your people.

Give up your leaders, too, and the memory of them: those who stood tall with raised fist and said "No" to being humiliated; those who taught that the people's ways were good, and that they must be remembered, even practised, now. Those people were no-good tricksters, and the wise god Christ has disarmed them now. Though their most potent weapons were their voices, he has bound them, humiliated them, destroyed them. Remember that Christ the god knows what is good for you.

You may still be tempted—by a friend's whisper, by a dream, by a scent on the wind or a rustle in the forest—to follow old ways. To feel yourself again a part of the earth and its skies, its rivers, its seasons. To move among your fellow creatures as one of them, finding your place alongside theirs. To remember the ancestors and their ways of belonging to the earth, to one another, to themselves. These are dark and immoral thoughts. They will feel right and good and life-giving, but that is because your body will always lie to you.

You must listen only to the god to whom you now belong, the god who has trodden the old ways under his boots. This letter is the reason why. Your every waking thought must now be obedience to his discipline. This you must learn to call life.

It was one of them, their very own prophet, who said, "Cretans are always liars, vicious brutes, lazy gluttons." That testimony is true.... To the pure all things are pure, but to the corrupt and unbelieving nothing is pure. Their very minds and consciences are corrupted.

Titus 1:12–13, 15

TOTALIZING

Lisa Martens

WHEN I READ Paul's words as I prepared for a sermon, I laughed. In a dry humour kind of way. More racism in the Bible. All the people from Crete are bad. More all-or-nothing language. Totalizing language.

Totalizing includes the "Alls" and the "Alwayses" and the "Everthings" and "Absolutes":

Never
Complete
Perpetual
Final
Truth
Absolute Truth
Inherently Wrong
Inherently Good
Pure
Pure Evil
Everyone
Everything
None
Forever
All of Them
All of Us
Only
Best
Perfect

All or
Nothing.

The religion of my childhood reinforced all-or-nothing thinking in a way that I've been recovering from ever since.

Paul wrote to Titus invoking all good, calling down all bad, and giving fervent instructions on how his co-worker should choose blameless and pure elders for the new church in Crete. But, in the case of this "Cretans are always liars" verse, it's a *Cretan* who said these things about Cretans.

Then again, it's a *non*-Cretan who *reported* that a Cretan said them.

A Cretan said mean, critical, totalizing things about themself. I do that to myself, sometimes. One day, in my 20s, I was having a hard time with some of the logistics and emotions of life. I made a joke that was harshly disparaging of myself, and the person I was with looked at me closely and didn't crack a smile.

"That was meant to be a joke," I said, deflated.

"I know," they said, quietly, after a long pause.

I cannot forget the feeling of mediated shame I felt for having been cruel to myself, or how seriously the person took me. I started more clearly noticing the effects of habitual self-insult in my life, and that habit lightened and shifted. Our words are part of what co-creates reality.

On the other hand, laughing at myself, making fun of my goof-ups, taking myself less seriously, and watching others do the same for themselves, is one of the more life-giving practices I know. All or nothing? *All or something?*

Paul wasn't from Crete. But he said that a Cretan—themself—said mean, critical, and totalizing things about themself and their people. Sometimes my family does that too.

At a recent gathering, one of my white relatives started talking about an Indigenous person they'd met who had talked about their own Indigenous family in a disparaging way. Until I conjured up the words to contradict and stop my relative, their anecdote went on to give evidence—using quotes from an Indigenous person—that Indigenous people are inherently uncivilized. My relative said those things, here, on this land.

A Cretan said mean, critical and totalizing things about their own people, and I feel my ability to critique my own people is important, as well.

I can speak to my own racism and the racism of the people I'm close to—the white Mennonites, for example—with more integrity than I can speak to the racism or other dis-eases of people further from me.

Here sit white Mennonites, on this land, taken from Indigenous people in unfair ways. We live our lives and make our money here, complicit in the theft of land and waterways. I type on a computer and absorb the warmth of a space heater, both powered by electricity from Pimicikamak Cree Nation, where damages to shorelines due to colonizer hydro dams have still not been healed. I drink and shower in the delicious water of Shoal Lake because an aqueduct was built there; that aqueduct displaced the Ojibway people who live at Shoal Lake 40, people who now have to boil all their water in order to enjoy that gift. This is why some who teach about power dynamics and racism use totalizing language and say there is no such thing as being neutral with regard to racism. For Settler colonizers, just walking along, plugging stuff in, and drinking the water is racist, no matter if we Settlers say mean things or not.

My head shakes as I reflect on Paul's words in Titus. But is there anything wrong with being a "lover of goodness"—the command Paul gives to potential elders of the church? My guess is the apostle and I might come to blows in a job interview. Yet, I'm not addicted to wine or overly greedy for gain (see verses 6–8). I do love goodness (on Wednesdays), and if anyone has accused me of debauchery, it's never been to my face. I want to be good. I want my people to be good and compassionate, and to do justice and reverse harm. And if the "totalizing" language of the Bible—or from other sources—helps boost people's desire for goodness, that might be okay.

My friend came back from a meeting about LGBTQ2 people being welcome (or not) in church and said: "There's lots of room for different opinions in this world, but when someone says my very existence, as a queer person, is wrong, I won't entertain that. Then they're wrong."

And then there's the totalizing language of the *United Nations Declaration on the Rights of Indigenous Peoples*, which the Truth and Reconciliation Commission of Canada asserts is the framework for reconciliation in this country:

...all doctrines, policies, and practices based on or advocating superiority of peoples or individuals on the basis of national origin or racial, religious, ethnic, or cultural differences are racist, scientifical-ly false, legally invalid, morally condemnable, and socially unjust... Indigenous peoples, in the exercise of their rights, should be free from discrimination of any kind...

One of my mentors at my therapy practicum likes to keep things open-ended and stay away from absolutes and finalities and totalizing language. So it's more remarkable (than it would be for some of us more hot-headed types) that this person still draws hard lines: No, homopho-bia is never okay. No, racism is never okay. Yes, non-discrimination is our industry standard. Some beliefs do too much harm to be okay.

Yet in other contexts, in other ways, totalizing language around goodness and perfect goodness, and purity, have their sad and neurotic sides. How many people who have suffered from depression or anxi-ety, and who do invisible or visible violence to themselves and others, have powerful and poisonous ideas of "perfect" and "good" embedded in their pain? For such people, who take the Bible seriously, to what degree has the Bible's totalizing, all-or-nothing language contributed to their difficulty?

Totalizing language. About Cretans, about Me, about Indigenous Peoples, about Mennonites, about Queer People, about Situations. I'm for it. I'm against it. I think it's pure evil. *Just kidding.* I think it's some-times wise to back up and explore the antidotes to totalizing. The

maybes
the not forevers,
the relentings,
the I don't knows
the meet-you-half-ways
the ways to live somewhere between the extremes we've touched
the ordinary compromises, and the sacred ones.

And still. There are times when totalizing language is what we need. It pushes forward our best and most just and beautiful hopes for our lives.

I am appealing to you for my child,
Onesimus, whose father I have
become during my imprisonment.
Formerly he was useless to you, but
now he is indeed useful both to
you and to me. I am sending him,
that is, my own heart, back to you.

Philemon 10–12

LET US IMAGINE

Miguel A. De La Torre

Swish. "Aauph!"
Swish. "Aauph!"

TAKING A DEEP BREATH, Onesimus, small in stature but muscular in frame, lifted his trusty machete high above his head as if reaching for the heavens. Then with a burst of raw energy, he swung it down hard to clear another patch of the unceasing sugar cane field which lay before him.

Swish.

As his machete made its mark, scattering tall thin cane to the four corners of the earth, he violently exhaled: "Aauph!"

In synchronized rhythm he continued this process, hour after hour, week after week, month after month, year after year. The work was exhausting. Swollen hands, bare feet full of bloody blisters, back soaked in sweat and dark black from the bruises of the whip, eyes red from averaging only three to four hours a night of sleep. Few Yoruba slaves live beyond seven years working under the unforgiving blistering sun which hangs high in the Cuban sky. Onesimus was being worked to death, for it was much cheaper to buy a new slave than to care for an existing one.

Swish. "Aauph!"
Swish. "Aauph!"

As if slashing a hot knife through a stick of butter, the cane field simply melted away before the terrifying brute strength of Onesimus. Memories of his tranquil home by the river Yewa — before his wife was raped and killed, before his small children were sold to a lecher — tormented his mind.

Swish. "Aauph!"
Swish. "Aauph!"

Never taking a break, never resting for a moment, Onesimus murmured silent prayers to his orisha Ogún, while he eternally laboured so white colonial masters could profit off the sweat of his brow.

When Onesimus disembarked from the huge wooden canoe where he was shackled and forced to exist in his vomit and manure for six weeks, he noticed what seemed to be a grotesque figure, oversized and pale, sitting in an elaborate golden chair, and wearing the garb of a great prince. As Onesimus and his compatriots struggled toward dry land, this creature sprinkled water upon them claiming they were now baptized, and thus Christians. If Onesimus had the slightest inclination he was being initiated into some new religion, no doubt he would reject it, as had Hatüey, the original inhabitant of the island who rebelled against the colonizers. When Hatüey was caught and offered salvation before being burned at the stake, he asked if colonizers went to heaven. When the good padre answered in the affirmative, the Taíno cacique said he would prefer to go to hell where he wouldn't see such cruel people.

Swish. "Aauph!"
Swish. "Aauph!"

As Onesimus's life drained from his being, he thought of escaping. Marrón communities existed in places like Viñales: communities comprised only of Africans and Indigenous people. If caught, he could expect to have his leg cut off as though it was a stalk of sugar cane, or his Achilles tendon removed. Rumours of castration, even being roasted to death circulated through the barracoons (slave living quarters). Better to die attempting to reach these safe havens than to die in the sugar fields, working in conditions that are worse than what the animals used to grind sugar cane are subject to.

Let us imagine Onesimus was to escape.

Let us imagine Onesimus failed to reach the Marrón community, and instead found refuge in the home of a Christian who took pity upon him and offered him sanctuary. Let's say that this Christian, whose name is Pablo, knew Onesimus's master, Filemón, a dear friend and fellow worker, someone for whom Pablo thanks God, someone for whom Pablo prays. Because Filemón and Pablo worship the God of empire, the God of the colonizer, the God of the slaveholders, the right thing to do is to return Onesimus to where he belongs. Pablo writes Filemón a letter stating:

> I am sending him—who is my very heart—back to you. I would have liked to keep him with me so that he could take your place in helping me while I am in chains for the gospel. Perhaps the reason he was separated from you for a little while was that you might have him back forever—no longer as a slave, but better than a slave, as a dear brother.

If you are Onesimus, what would you do? Return to Filemón, your brother in Christ, and continue serving him? Or would you kill Pablo before he raises the alarm and continue your journey to find the Marrónes?

If they had been thinking of the land that they had left behind, they would have had opportunity to return. But as it is, they desire a better country, that is, a heavenly one. Therefore God is not ashamed to be called their God; indeed, he has prepared a city for them.

Hebrews 11:15–16

WE SAW OUR GRANDCHILDREN

Sara Anderson, with teachings from Edward Benton-Banai

WE CAME INTO BEING by the thoughts of Gitchi Manitou, the Great Mystery, the Creator. Grandfather Sun and Grandmother Moon, Giizis and Niibagiizis, this is what *nindinawemagunidoog* (our relatives) call us. When Gitchi Manitou called Mother Earth into being, all things in the universe were given original instructions; how we are to act, what our purpose is, how we are to look. I, Grandfather Sun, provide light, warmth, and life so that all on Mother Earth may be. I, Grandmother Moon, guide all women and direct the vast waters so that all on Mother Earth may be. We keep watch over all; these are our original instructions.

Since time immemorial, we have watched our grandchildren, the Anishinaabe. We saw them receive their original instructions — how they are to act, what their purpose is, how they are to look — so that they could live in a good way (*mino biimadiziwiin*). We saw the *niizhwaas-wi niigawnakeg* (seven prophets) who came to the Anishinaabe when they were living a full and peaceful life. We heard as the seven prophets left seven predictions in seven fires (*niizhwaaswi ishkodekwaan*) of what the future would bring. We watched as these fires came to pass. We are the witnesses who will continue to watch and carry out our original instructions, so that all on Mother Earth may be.

We watched as the first prophet said to the people:

In the time of the First Fire, the Anishinaabe nation will rise up and follow the Sacred Shell of the Midewiwin Lodge. The Midewiwin Lodge will serve as a rallying point for the people, and its traditional ways will be the source of much strength. The sacred shells (*megis*) will lead the way to the chosen ground of the Anishinaabe. You are to look for a turtle-shaped island that is linked to the purification of the Earth. You will find such an island at the beginning and end of your journey. There will be seven stopping places along the way. You will know that the chosen ground has been reached when you come to a land where food grows on water. If you do not move, you will be destroyed.

We saw our grandchildren, the Anishinaabe, divide over the words of this prophet. Many did not believe him, and they decided to stay in the East by the great sea where they thought there were enough *mushkiiki-winun* (medicines) to keep away all sickness. But those who believed in the words of this prophet began a great migration.

And so we, Grandfather Sun and Grandmother Moon, saw the words of the first prophet come to pass. Then we watched as the second and third prophets said to the people:

You will know the Second Fire because at this time the nation will be camped by a large body of water. In this time, the direction of the Sacred Shell will be lost. The Midewiwin will diminish in strength. A boy will be born to point the way back to the traditional ways. He will show the direction to the stepping stones to the future of the Anishinaabe people.

In the Third Fire, the Anishinaabe will find the path to their chosen ground, a land in the West to which they must move their families. This will be the land where food grows on water.

We saw the Anishinaabe look for the island shaped like a turtle. And then we saw our granddaughter receive a gift, a *bawaajigan* (dream) from Gitchi Manitou. In this dream, she saw herself on the back of a turtle in the water, whose tail pointed East and whose face pointed West. We then watched the Elders instruct the people to go out and explore the rivers heading West where they would find this island. The Anishinaabe, our grandchildren, performed many ceremonies to prepare and cleanse themselves. And then we saw them make their way along the Great River, stopping many times as the Sacred Shell instructed them. We saw that at the beginning, our grandchildren upheld the instructions to keep the Manitou Ishkode (The Sacred Fire) alive along this journey.

As time passed, we witnessed many births and deaths among our grandchildren. We saw that some of the Anishinaabe began to wander away from the teachings of the Midewiwin Lodge; they did not perform the ceremonies. Soon, only the Elders were left to keep the Manitou Ishkode lit. We then saw that a grandson was born, one who had a dream of stones that led across the water.

Our grandson showed the people the way to the stones — the islands — which led across the water. We saw that the Anishinaabe followed the boy and continued their journey towards the land where wild rice grew plentifully and where our grandchildren would again practice the ways of the Midewiwin Lodge. And so we, Grandfather Sun and Grandmother Moon, saw the words of the second and third prophets come to pass.

We watched as the fourth prophets, two-who-came-as-one, said to the people:

> You will know the future of our people by what face the Light-skinned Race wears. If they come wearing the face of *niikonnisiwin* (brotherhood), then there will come a time of wonderful change for generations to come. They will bring new knowledge and articles that can be joined with the knowledge of this country. In this way two nations will join to make a mighty nation. This new nation will be joined by two more so that the four will form the mightiest nation of all. You will know the face of brotherhood if the Light-skinned Race comes carrying no weapons, if they come bearing only their knowledge and a handshake.
>
> Beware if the Light-skinned Race comes wearing the face of *niboowin* (death). You must be careful because the face of brotherhood and the face of death look very much alike. If they come carrying a weapon... beware. If they come in suffering... they could fool you. Their hearts may be filled with greed for the riches of this land. If they are indeed your brothers, let them prove it. Do not accept them in total trust. You shall know that the face they wear is the one of death if the rivers run with poison and fish become unfit to eat. You shall know them by these many things.

We saw our grandchildren meet the people of the Light-skinned Race. We saw that some came with a handshake, but many came with weapons and greed in their hearts. And thus we observed the words of the fourth prophets come to pass.

Then the fifth prophet said to the people:

> In the time of the Fifth Fire, there will come a time of great struggle that will grip the lives of all Native people. At the waning of this Fire, there will come among the people one who holds a promise of great joy and salvation. If the people accept this promise of a new way and abandon the old teachings, then the struggle of the Fifth Fire will be with the people for many generations. The promise that comes will prove to be a false promise. All those who accept this promise will cause the near destruction of the people.

We saw the Anishinaabe walk into this great struggle. We saw that some of our grandchildren believed the words of the Mukadayikonyag (the Black Coats). Our grandchildren abandoned the ancient ways and forgot their original instructions.

We saw many generations of our grandchildren gripped by this struggle. And so we, Grandfather Sun and Grandmother Moon, witnessed the words of the fifth prophet come to pass.

We watched as the sixth prophet said to the people:

> In the time of the Sixth Fire it will be evident that the promise of the Fifth Fire came in a false way. Those deceived by this promise will take their children away from the teachings of the *chi'-ah-ya-og'* (the Elders). Grandsons and granddaughters will turn against the Elders. In this way the Elders will lose their reason for living... they will lose their purpose in life. At this time a new sickness will come among the people. The balance of many people will be disturbed. The cup of life will almost be spilled.

We saw our grandchildren fracture. We saw children taken away from their families and saw that grandsons and granddaughters turned against their Elders. We saw that many of our grandchildren lost their purpose. We saw new sicknesses creep into every corner of their lives. We saw that the cup of life turned bitter and became the cup of grief for some of our grandchildren. And so we, Grandfather Sun and Grandmother Moon, witnessed the words of the sixth prophet come to pass.

We watched as the seventh prophet, who was young and had a strange light in his eyes, said to the people:

> In the time of the Seventh Fire an Oshkibimadiziig (a New People) will emerge. They will retrace their steps to find what was left by the trail. Their steps will take them to the Elders who they will ask to guide them on their journey. But many of the Elders will have fallen asleep. They will awaken to this new time with nothing to offer. Some of the Elders will be silent out of fear. Some of the Elders will be silent because no one will ask anything of them. The New People will have to be careful in how they approach the Elders. The task of the New People will not be easy.
>
> If the New People will remain strong in their quest, the Waterdrum of the Midewiwin Lodge will again sound its voice. There will be a rebirth of the Anishinaabe nation and a rekindling of old flames. The Sacred Fire will be lit again.
>
> It is at this time that the Light-skinned Race will be given a choice between two roads. If they choose the right road, then the Seventh Fire will light the Eighth and Final Fire—an eternal Fire of peace, love, brotherhood, and sisterhood.

We see our grandchildren, the Oshkibimadiziig (the New People), beginning to emerge. We watch as the New People turn back to their original instructions and seek to live in a good way (*mino biimadiziwiin*). We observe as the Light-skinned Race continues to be divided about which road they will choose. We wonder if the Eighth Fire, a fire of peace, love, brotherhood, and sisterhood, will be lit. And so we will wait for the words of the seventh prophet to come to pass.

We, Grandfather Sun and Grandmother Moon, are the witnesses who have watched and who will continue to watch. We carry out our original instructions so that all on Mother Earth may be.

Excerpts from The Mishomis Book *by Edward Benton-Banai used with kind permission from University of Minnesota Press.*

Come now, you rich people,
weep and wail for the miseries
that are coming to you.

James 5:1

RIPE FOR JUDGMENT

Sheila Klassen-Wiebe

Hey, you! Yeah, you — the white settler, (neo)colonial,
     fur trader turned
     industrial-agribusiness-commercial logger:
Do you know your fortunes are about to turn?
Rant and rail, weep and wail.
No good that will do.

The sentence has come down.

That black crude investment, blood of the earth,
will burst from its confining steel veins, giving
slick sheen to pristine waters.
     Fish belly-up and gasping;
     you too drink the poisoned water.

Hectares upon rolling hectares of shining gold will parch and perish,
     million dollar combines silent in the field
     as drought conquers the land.
You have taken more than you need,
hoarded for yourself today what could sustain your children tomorrow.
But it's running through your fingers like sand
     or maybe dust/rust,
     rotting, molding, withering, fraying,
     eating your life like a cancer,
     "nothing gold can stay."[†]

Treasure stored up in dirty stocks and bonds
will be your "treasure" on the day of reckoning.
"For where your treasure is, there will your heart be also."‡

Weekly pay cheques meted out meticulously,
minimum wage and not a penny more for all those
      migrant workers picking peaches,
        factory labourers in mind-numbing lines,
          "dirty Indians" hoeing fields of sugar beets
              on lands your ancestors loved, and stole.
Health and dental care not your problem, so you say,
hearts hard and ears deaf to the cries, the petitions,
the tired despair of workers
you've used and discarded.
Listen! Can't you hear them?

God is not deaf!
From fields and factories, the cries rise up to Lord Sabaoth.
From inner city tenements and remote reserves,
their cries batter the doors of heaven.
And the Creator opens the door.
From ancient times this Divine Warrior has battled
  injustice and oppression.
The Lord of Hosts has heard.
The Lord of Hosts will hear...and hear...and here
will act with justice once again.

You rearrange rivers and lakes
to feed your hydroelectric need-greed,
      drunk on the power of those humming lines,
        oblivious to the destruction of traditional lifeways, sacred sites,
          wildlife habitats.
You have water slides, water parks, just-turn-on-the-tap water to drink,
      yet Indigenous neighbours, just down the road

† poem by Robert Frost, "Nothing Gold Can Stay"
‡ Matthew 6:21

die with an 18-year-long boil water advisory,
drink water from throw-away plastic,
suffer mercury poisoning from the Settler mill.

But you live!
in gated communities,
crisp new suburbs of cookie-cutter condos,
walk-through pantries and walk-in closets,
marble countertops and maple cabinets,
> as reports of substandard housing
> in remote communities
> play on your flat screen TV:
> "Eighteen people live in a shack with
> no indoor plumbing, mold on the walls...."

You are ripe for judgment.

You have twisted the flat steel blade of the law to serve yourself
and let justice die.
You have murdered the innocent
> with your insipid concern for suicides among Indigenous
> youth,
> with your hardness of heart for prisons full of Indigenous
> casualties of "the system,"
> with your apathetic silence about missing and murdered
> Indigenous women,
> with your cultural genocide in residential schools, legacy
> ongoing and unforgotten.
How can they resist?

¤

Ah, but these words, brother James, are surely not for us good Christian
folk?
Surely your audience is elsewhere,
> the big shots who work in government, legal offices,
> corporations,

the callous who don't give a cup of cold water in the name of
   Christ,
the irreligious who don't pray your kingdom come.
Surely they are not for us.
Are they?

Slaves, accept the authority of your masters with all deference, not only those who are kind and gentle but also those who are harsh. For it is a credit to you if, being aware of God, you endure pain while suffering unjustly.

1 Peter 2:18–19

SURVIVAL SPACE

Chris Budden

HE FELT GOOD as he walked out of the overnight lockup. There was something satisfying in knowing he had the courage to stand up for other people's rights. Not that it was a huge thing. If he was honest, his efforts were almost game-like, even calculated. He wanted his actions to match his convictions. He wanted to achieve a bit of justice, something with a cost, something that got his skin in the game. But well-off, white, middle-aged men aren't treated that badly, even when they protest and make a nuisance of themselves. Indeed—and it didn't do his ego much good to admit this—those in control likely allowed such protest as a way to show that debate, discussion, and demonstration were possible in society. It created an illusion of "people power."

He also knew that his "justice issues" were not merely issues for the people whose struggles he joined. They were matters of life and sometimes death. This was about survival and dignity. About languages not going extinct, cultures being rescued from the oppressor's shame, and the recovery of land.

Which is why he sometimes wondered, as he did now (settling into his wife's car for the short drive home), why the people were not always at the protests. And why they sometimes argued for the less risky options and the less confrontational ways forward. There was a level of fear which he simply did not understand and wasn't even sure he believed was necessary.

Occasionally, he got a glimpse of a different world, one nowhere near as safe and secure as his. He would see the racism people had to deal with, the threats of violence against families, the financial risks that protest and resistance brought, the dissimilar ways that police would deal with them, and the courts too.

He came to understand that, for many, this life was struggle, not liberation. Survival, not freedom.

Maybe that's why so many of the people chose to fit in and conform to society in ways that surprised him. How else do you explain why they'd say it was good to obey the authorities? How else do you explain why those in shitty-jobs-that-barely-pay-enough-to-live refuse to allow unions at work, and do everything they're asked by their bosses? Why so many men send their wives to police stations when there's an issue, rather than go themselves?

It's as if they want to fly under the radar, not be noticed, and build their lives as best as they can. Who wants graffiti all over their house, to be spat on in the streets, to be mocked in the media, to bury children because it's too-much-effort-to-live, to fight for identity in an overwhelmingly white world, and fill up the jails? Who can take on ideological battles when the priority is to keep families fed and government officials off one's back?

Maybe people need to find their hope in other less obvious spaces, away from the public eye. Maybe in that survival space, stories of the suffering of Jesus, the presence of God in human form, was helpful and life giving?

It was in that crucified, nonresistant presence, where the early church, so pressed by colonial powers, found something full of promise. That right there, in the very heart of Sacred Life, was a goodness that knew suffering—that stands beside and values and affirms people, that denies empire its legitimacy. God knew, in God's very body, all wounds. To share the suffering of Jesus in the face of oppression and power was better than being alone and without hope. Perhaps that's why so many First Peoples in Australia identify with the witness of Jesus.

Maybe that is life. Maybe that is better than using the power of a community aligned with empire to "fix" things. That would be just another form of power over one's lives. Just another false dependency.

In the last days scoffers will come… saying, "Where is the promise of his coming? For ever since our ancestors died, all things continue as they were from the beginning of creation!" They deliberately ignore this fact, that by the word of God heavens existed long ago and an earth was formed out of water and by means of water, through which the world of that time was deluged with water and perished. But by the same word the present heavens and earth have been reserved for fire, being kept until the day of judgment and destruction of the godless.

2 Peter 3:3–7

PETER'S LETTER TO CANADIAN CHRISTIANS

Steve Heinrichs

TO THE FRIENDS living in the colonized lands of the Salish, Mi'kmaq, and Innu. This is Peter, follower of the poor Christ, in prison on the West Coast. I write because the time is urgent. Some say, "The end of all things is near" (1 Peter 4:7). Some say, "Eternity is being determined now." Some say, if the idols of capital continue unabated, we will "exceed the threshold of 1.5 degrees in 10 years."

I don't know what the future holds. But I do know that we are not "aliens and exiles" to God's love and the world's grace (1 Peter 2:11). What I know is that we are citizens of creation, and we must defend the "heavens and earth that are reserved for fire" (2 Peter 3:7). What I know is that the plans of the proud need to be dismantled and history launched into holiness, for it is written, "Seek justice and correct oppression" (Isaiah 1:17).

The crucified across "Canada" have sounded the alarm. Host peoples and waters, trees, and fish have lifted their voices in united lament: "Our common home is in peril!" They've summoned big business and urged the affluent to "Cease and desist your extractive ways!"

Yet, the establishment, driven by voracious visions of growth, have shutdown ears and suspended hearts. And so have most Christians. Addicted to throw-away culture, numbed by Netflix, distracted by dreams of the next marvellous vacation, they sit idly by, offering tacit blessing to the status quo.

Is there hope? Can God move us out of climate darkness and into a measure of light (1 Peter 2:9)? Will a remnant of the church join the bruised and battered who are standing up for sister Earth?

For Christ's sake, we pray: Move us into his steps, into his example (1 Peter 2:21)!

> He came preaching peace,
> good news of God's reign.
> He came preaching challenge,
> contesting the reign of death.
> He was put to death by the powers,
> "but made alive in the spirit" (1 Peter 3:18).

Remember, friends:

Our Lord was killed not because he helped the poor, not because he showed mercy to the suffering, but because he confronted the rich and ruling authorities. You simply can't go around saying hard things like he did and expect to live long.

Remember, friends:

God has called us to do good in the form of this Christ. Earth is being un-created, and the forces of the fossil economy—oil corporations, near-sighted governments, free-market churches—must be challenged. Yes, we do good through gentle lifeways. Yes, we do good by living simply and alternatively. But, we also do good by denouncing the gods that are consuming God's world.

If we do, we will suffer. We will get pushed out of churches. We will get pushed into prisons. Yet, if we endure, we will receive the approval of the One who raised Christ from the dead (1 Peter 1:21).

Stand fast in God's grace, beloved. And stand up.

And the kings of the earth, who committed fornication and lived in luxury with her, will weep and wail over her when they see the smoke of her burning; they will stand far off, in fear of her torment, and say, "Alas, alas, the great city, Babylon, the mighty city! For in one hour your judgment has come."

Revelation 18:9–10

O CEDAR TREE, CLAP YOUR HANDS

Wes Howard-Brook

WHEN WHITE PEOPLE first harvested salmon in the Salish Sea to feed factory workers over in England, the daily catch lined the dock waist high. Now there are few salmon in the overfished, acidified, and too warm waters of "Puget Sound."

When white people first began harvesting trees on Tiger Mountain to build the Great City, Seattle, the firs and cedars that covered the hills reached over 200 feet into the sky. Now, one old-growth tree remains.

When white people first arrived, the creeks and the woods overflowed with otters, beavers, cougar, bear, coyote, and deer. The otters and beavers are totally gone. And in 34 years, I've never seen a cougar.

¤

And I heard from the silence of the forest a loud voice, proclaiming for all to hear:

"Fallen, fallen is the global economy! For all peoples have drunk from its alluring cup, and the one percent have grown rich from the power of its luxury!"

And I heard a different voice calling out, "Come out, my people, so that you are no longer enriched by the massive sin done to earth and her inhabitants! The global economy has collapsed, and with it all the institutions upon which it relied: the great banks, the International Monetary Fund, the lobbying firms and corporate media!"

And then I saw the corporate elite wailing and weeping, crying, "Alas, our markets are no more!" And the banksters and their companions broke out in terrible lament, as all upon which they relied was no more. And the voice continued: "Alas, Amazon and Starbucks, Microsoft and Costco are no more! All the endless items available at a click will never be found again!"

But then I heard another voice, calling out to the earth: "Celebrate, you earth-creatures, for Creator has done this for you! You have been set free from your captivity to empire! Be fruitful and multiply! Re-fill the earth and celebrate your release!"

And as time passed, I saw it.

Douglas fir, Western red cedar, and thimbleberry bushes grew and multiplied. The carbon-soaked sky began to sigh in relief as the air's balance and harmony were restored. And as the sky cooled, the water did too, and overheated salmon splashed happily in the fresh waters of Issaquah Creek and Lake Sammamish again. And as carbon-fuelled traffic ceased, asphalt cracked and opened up to fireweed and salal bushes and foxgloves. Then I heard the words of a Coast Salish song from ancient days, ringing out in the forest:

O, cedar tree, clap your hands and dance with me!
Way ai ay, way ai ay, way ai ay ai ay ai ay!

And many buildings, now abandoned, became covered with vines, and birds made their nests in them. And slowly but surely, rodents and mammals, both large and small, smiled and grinned at the change all around. They came out of hiding, had babies and cubs, and filled the forests with their songs and growls.

And the two-legged ones who remained celebrated as they relearned the knowledge of the land and made friends with the deer, bear, and coyotes. And I heard another voice, shouting out, "Rejoice, all you whose citizenship is in Creator's realm! Never again will our watershed-home be under the chokehold of empire and its greed! For all is now well, and all manner of things are well, and all will be well, for the Creator has taken authority over earth, and reigns forever and ever! Oh, yes!"

I saw no temple in the city, for its temple is the Lord God the Almighty and the Lamb. And the city has no need of sun or moon to shine on it, for the glory of God is its light, and its lamp is the Lamb. The nations will walk by its light, and the kings of the earth will bring their glory into it.

Revelation 21:22–24

TURTLE ISLAND RENEWED

Dan Epp-Tiessen

THEN I SAW a renewed heaven and a renewed earth, for the old order of things had passed away. And the sea was no more—the sea that brought the colonizers' ships, soldiers, guns, and diseases, and their slaves, and their dreams of wealth, plunder, and domination. The sea which was used to strip Turtle Island of its riches—its furs, lumber, fish, agricultural goods, silver, and gold—will no longer be available as a highway of exploitation.

I saw the renewed Turtle Island lovingly fashioned by the Creator's hands, and I heard a loud voice thundering from the sky, "See, the home of God is among humans, and among the plants, and the creatures, and the ecosystems, all across Turtle Island and across the entire globe. Creator will live with them as their God, their sustainer and healer, so that they will never again be harmed or go astray. Creator will wipe every tear from their eyes and every scar from the landscape. Death will be no more. Mourning and crying and pain will be no more. Economic exploitation and oppression will be no more. Colonialism and its painful legacy will be no more. Greed and ecological destruction will be no more. Militarism with its callous disregard for lives, resources, and ecosystems will be no more. Racism, sexism, exceptionalism, and all other *isms* that alienate and harm will be no more. For the old ways of doing things have passed away."

And the Creator of all said, "See, I am making all things new. Bead these words into a Wampum belt, for my promise is trustworthy and true. I am the beginning and the end, from sunrise to sunset. I am the four directions. To all who are thirsty I give water as a gift from the spring of the water of life. Those who hold fast in difficult times and live in keeping with my promises will inherit my good future, and I will be their God and they will be my children and my relations. But those who resist my plans for healing and renewal and continue to exploit, wage war, pollute, and hoard, those who continue to pledge allegiance to the false gods of nationalism, militarism, and consumerism, they will all be abandoned to the consequences of their choices."

Then one of Creator's Spirits said to me, "Come, I will show you Creator's dream for the renewed Turtle Island." The Spirit carried me away to a high mountain. And as I looked out over Turtle Island, I saw that it was filled with the Creator's glory and presence. All the plants, animals, and ecosystems were thriving. On the maples, cedars, birches, and spruce were signs naming and welcoming all the tribes, peoples, and nations of Turtle Island. And the bison again roamed the prairie, alongside the waving fields of wheat. And flocks of passenger pigeons again darkened the skies. And the waters again teemed with salmon, trout, walleye, and cod.

The Creator's Spirit had a fishing line to measure Turtle Island. It was perfectly round, stretching equal distance in the four directions. Its dimensions were perfect, and its many ecosystems provided abundantly for all God's creatures to live and thrive.

I saw no buildings of worship in Turtle Island, because the Creator and the Son-Daughter had come to live in the land, and they were always present to be respected and praised. There was no need for artificial lighting in the renewed creation, because Creator was its light, and the Son-Daughter reflected Creator's rays into every dark space. The peoples and creatures of Turtle Island walked in the Creator's light and rejoiced in the opportunity to offer gratitude and praise. There was no need for fences, walls, or boundaries to keep out danger, because Creator had purified the world of all wrongdoing and restored all those who stood in the way of Creator's healing purposes. There was no need for fences and walls to keep out undesirables, because Creator intends Turtle Island to be home for all.

Then the Spirit showed me the river of the water of life, flowing from the sacred fire of the Creator and the Son-Daughter, through the centre of Turtle Island. On either side of the river grew the tree of life, transplanted from primordial time, providing abundant fruit in every season of the year. The leaves of the tree were for the healing of the nations, and the creatures, and the plants, and all our relations. No more pain, or sorrow, or evil would be found in Turtle Island, because Creator and the Son-Daughter were present. All saw them and rejoiced. All gave gifts of praise and thanksgiving.

This is what Creator's good future looks like. Blessed are those who live in keeping with this vision.

WE NEED OUR LANDS

Sylvia McAdam

"These are our lands, right nohkom?"

I'M TAKING MY GRANDCHILDREN to our ancestral lands, lands on which we have hunted and lived since the beginning of time. As we drive up, I can feel the peace that this beloved place offers so generously. My people's territory is breathtakingly beautiful. Yet along with that comfort, I sense much heartache.

"These are our lands, right nohkom?"

My grandchildren are playing with sand, holding rich handfuls high and letting the grains run gently through their fingers. Half asking, half telling, they look at me—"These are our lands, right nohkom?" "Yes," I answer, "these are our lands." They continue on with their play, exploring as I once did, and as their ancestors must have done as they too enjoyed the solace and solitude of this place. As I watch, I know my grandchildren will protect these lands, just as I am doing. Just as my father did. Just as his father did. They will defend these lands as so many generations of my people have done since the first Settlers came.

Time and again, the Original Nations have reminded Settler peoples that we have been present on these lands since the beginning, and that we are still here. We lovingly call our lands Turtle Island. And we know these lands the same way we know all our relatives—intimately, with love and profound respect. I am raising my grandchildren so that they know who we *nêhiyawak* are, that they know their lands and care for them. And so it's with an incredibly heavy heart that I know this "fight" to defend and protect our lands against ongoing colonial theft and resource extraction will not end with me. It will continue for as long as the colonizer covets these lands for profit, for as long as they see mere resources, instead of living relatives.

That violent way of viewing the world is bound up with the Doctrine of Discovery, a complex legal tradition that arose in the West during the medieval period, a settler colonial tradition in which the Church played a leading role. The Doctrine of Discovery has been around at least since the 11th century and the Crusades, but it took on hellish strength in the 15th century, when a series of papal bulls were created to justify Christian conquest. Among them was the 1455 *Romanus Pontifex*, a papal bull which sanctified the seizure of newly "discovered" lands and encouraged the enslavement of native peoples. Then, in 1493, Pope Alexander VI issued *Inter Caetera*, a definitive statement giving Spain title to the Americas. It is through this church law that the infamous explorer (or land speculator) Christopher Columbus was given his royal prerogatives to subdue, convert or kill the barbarians, and to assert the Monarchy's title to the land.

> Among other works well pleasing to the Divine Majesty... this assuredly ranks highest... [that] the Catholic faith... be everywhere increased and spread... and that barbarous nations be overthrown and brought to the faith itself... [We] give, grant, and assign to you and your heirs and successors... all islands and mainlands... discovered and to be discovered towards the west and south.

With his royal prerogatives in hand, Columbus arrived to the far south of Turtle Island. His first act was rich with Christian symbolism: He planted a sword into the soil and invoked a Christian chant that baptized the lands. This chant was a symbolic act of asserting sovereignty and dominance over Indigenous peoples and territories and all that came with it. This seemingly simple act—a symbolic Christian ritual—set in motion a series of horrific events still felt today in American and Canadian courts, laws, and policies.

In 1497, Britain decided that it too could join the discovery venture, making sovereign claims in the Americas without violating the Church's rules and regulations with Spain and Portugal. And so Henry VII gifted explorer John Cabot (c. 1450 – 1500) with a charter that empowered him

> …to sail to all parts, regions and coasts of the eastern, western and northern sea…to find, discover, and investigate whatsoever… regions or provinces of the heathens and infidels, in whatsoever part of the world placed, which before this time were unknown to all Christians.

We're not exactly sure where Cabot landed—likely in Newfoundland or Cape Breton. He had no contact with the local Indigenous peoples. And he didn't stay long. Captain and crew simply replenished their water supplies and planted flags, which claimed the land for the King of England and recognized the authority of the Church. Yet it's at that very moment—when those flags are planted—that colonial common law claims that "the sovereignty of the Crown crystallized." It was at that very moment that the British Monarchy took possession of the lands all along the eastern seaboard of Turtle Island, and the "Indians" with it. (That's right, Indigenous peoples became property of the Crown!) And it's because of that moment, and the death-dealing legal and religious traditions that produced and sustained that moment, that all of us Indigenous peoples in "Canada" are under an Indian Act (first passed in 1876), as well as ongoing colonial law and policy.

I live in Treaty 6 territory. When that sacred agreement was made at Fort Carton and Fort Pitt back in 1876, hereditary Chiefs repeatedly asked the Treaty commissioner Alexander Morris, "We have heard our lands are sold, we don't like it, and no one has asked us—are they sold?" Each time, Morris—the representative of the Queen—reassured the group: "The land belongs to you. It has not been sold." It was based on that assurance that Treaty 6 negotiations continued on, and a covenant between Creator, First Nations, and the Crown was agreed to.

And yet despite those "sweet promises," a web of lies immediately followed that Treaty-making. Lies that form and perpetuate a colonial vision of Treaty history that has become the dominant "truth," Canada's "truth." One of the most damaging falsehoods that Settlers have accepted is the idea that Indigenous nations ceded and surrendered our lands and resources. We *nêhiyawak*, however, have no words in our language for "cede and surrender." We did not cede or surrender anything.

Today, we are told (endlessly so), that we are in a state of "reconciliation." It's frustrating to try and keep up with the contradictory actions of the colonizer. One moment, it's "Let's get along." The next moment, it's "We're building a pipeline here, no matter what you say." Isn't this what an abusive relationship looks like? It's either a honeymoon phase, with lots of good words and affection, or the explosive stage with ultimatums and threats of force...or very real acts of force and violence. Either way, we are wards of Canada. The grassroots don't have real input—sometimes any input—when decisions are made that impact our lives and our lands, like the

- Indian residential schools (ca. 1870s–1970s);
- pass and permit system (1885–1945);
- Natural Resource Transfer Act (1930);
- Sugar Beet Policy (1940s–80s);
- 60's Scoop;
- Comprehensive Land Claims process (1973 onwards);
- First Nations Governance Act (2002); and
- First Nations Financial Transparency Act (2013).

The list can go on. And, to the despair and anger of so many, it does.

If we are to move forward toward any genuine reconciliation, we must look to the grassroots. They understand what needs to happen in order for Indigenous peoples to survive and thrive. They know what we need in order to honour the spirit and intent of the Treaties. And foundational to the grassroots Indigenous vision is a recovery of land. As my good friend and mentor, the late Arthur Manuel (*Secwepemc Nation*) said, "Reparation of land precedes reconciliation." I couldn't agree more.

Colonization has resulted in overwhelming dispossession of land, dignity, and well-being. It has created dependency, dehumanization, and systemic structures of oppression and domination. These are the pillars that form and sustain the relationship between colonizer and the colonized.

Settlers need to understand that the United Nations has repeatedly challenged and condemned colonization in all its manifestations. In 1943, Articles 73 and 74 of the *United Nations Charter* summoned imperial powers to the work of facilitating self-government in their respective colonies. In 1960, the *Declaration on the Granting of Independence to Colonial Countries and Peoples* repudiated "the subjection of peoples" as a "denial of human rights" (Article 1), declaring that "all peoples have the right to self-determination" (Article 2), and that "immediate steps shall be taken...to transfer all powers to the peoples of those territories" that have not achieved independence (Article 5). Then in 2007, the nations of the world embraced the *Declaration on the Rights of Indigenous Peoples*—the most comprehensive recognition of the inherent rights of the world's 370 million Indigenous peoples—which repudiated colonialism by providing a blueprint for decolonization and reconciliation.

Why has the United Nations condemned colonization? "Because the moment you dispossess someone of their land and make them dependent upon the colonizer," says Arthur Manuel, "you create a person willing to fight to be free and independent again. In this way, colonialism is against world peace."

We all need to condemn colonialism. We all need to collectively work at decolonization. One of the first ways to do that work is to seek to understand the language of colonial domination, and then unmask it. Consider the following quote from the 1990 Supreme Court of Canada case, Regina (Queen) v. Sparrow:

> It is worth recalling that while British policy towards the native population was based on respect for their right to occupy their traditional lands... there was from the outset never any doubt that sovereignty and legislative power, and indeed the underlying title, to such lands vested in the Crown.

The phrase, "underlying title," is nothing but the Doctrine of Discovery. "Underlying title" is a claim to radical title—ultimate ownership. It's the "crystallization" of Crown sovereignty that happened when Cabot baptized Turtle Island with his imperial presence and legal fictions. The British Crown, and Canada as the successor colonial state, have acted on this presumption from day one of "discovery" until now to assert that they are the ones with definitive jurisdiction over these lands, despite the prevalent rhetoric of "Nation-to-Nation" relation-ships. This colonial vision is reflected in the preamble of the Canadian Constitution which states, "…whereas such a Union would conduce to the Welfare of the Provinces *and promote the Interests of the British Empire*" (emphasis added).

What does it mean to promote the interests of the British Empire? It means to enforce the Doctrine of Discovery for the sake of federal and provincial settler governments. It means carrying on the gross ex-ploitation, extraction, and plunder of the lands and "resources" of Turtle Island to benefit the Crown at all costs, turning an indifferent eye to the living Treaty promises and the real sovereignty of Indigenous peoples and nations.

As each year goes by, I see oil and gas exploration getting closer and closer to my family's hunting lands that are supposed to be protected by Treaty 6. The province of Saskatchewan, with the sanction of the Natural Resources Transfer Act, has issued permits for logging compa-nies to haul away our trees. The trees are gone now and they will not come back in my lifetime. The devastation is generational, and my heart aches. So long as the deceit and legal fiction of "underlying title" exists, I know that efforts to defend and protect these lands will not end with my generation.

In order for reconciliation to be realized, a significant contingent of Settler Canadians will need to push their State (and challenge them-selves) to dismantle these colonial myths. And then these same Settlers will need to organize and fight with us, so that we can get our lands back—enough land so that we can thrive. (At present, you can fit all First Nations land in Canada into the Navajo reservation, and still have half of that reservation leftover.) Our freedom and liberation—not just as Indigenous peoples, but all of us—depends on land reparation.

Unsettling the Word is a collection of courageous writings that in-vites all those who benefit from the Christian Doctrine of Discovery to make concerted effort to abolish the systems that have been cre-ated by it. *Unsettling the Word* summons those who have been shaped and impacted by the Judeo-Christian tradition (for good or for ill, by choice or by force), to not simply grapple intellectually with the prob-lems of settler colonialism, to not merely contemplate the promise of decolonization, but to step up and act. As the contributors make plain, settler colonialism is not over. It's an ever-present structure that lives and moves and has its being today.

For that reason, what we urgently need is a growing group of women and men who will take what they've learned from this text and bring it out to the streets and into the land: women and men who are so unsettled by what they have discovered that they will rise up and join growing Indigenous-led movements in Canada, the U.S., and beyond; women and men who will struggle for a decolonization that centres on the repatriation of Indigenous lands. Will you do that? My freedom, your freedom, my grandchildren's freedom, and the lands' freedom all depend on it.

CONTRIBUTORS

SARA ANDERSON lives and works on Anishinaabeg (Algonquin) territory in Ottawa, Ontario. Of Métis and German Mennonite ancestry, Sara works for KAIROS Canada in the role of Blanket Exercise Regional Coodinator and is a member of Ottawa Mennonite Church.

RALPH ARMBRUSTER-SANDOVAL is a Professor in the Chicana/o Studies Department at the University of California, Santa Barbara — traditional Chumash territory — whose foci include social movements, racial studies, Latin American studies, and liberation theology. Ralph is married and has two children, Sol and Sky.

CHERYL BEAR is Nadleh Whut'en from the Dakelh Nation and Dumdenyoo Clan (Bear clan) in central British Columbia. A community leader, band councillor, and theologian, Cheryl is also an award-winning singer-songwriter who seeks to share Indigenous life — the joy, sorrow, faith, and journey — through story and song.

DARRIN W. SNYDER BELOUSEK is a member of Salem Mennonite Church in Elida, Ohio — traditional territory of the Shawnee. A teacher in professional ethics at Ohio Northern University, Darrin is the author of *Atonement, Justice, and Peace* (2012) and *The Road That I Must Walk: A Disciple's Journey* (2014). He also served, from 2012–2018, as executive director of Bridgefolk, a Mennonite-Catholic ecumenical organization based at St. John's Abbey in Collegeville, Minnesota.

ROSE MARIE BERGER, a Catholic poet and writer, is a senior associate editor at *Sojourners* magazine. She has lived for more than 30 years in Washington, D.C., in the Anacostia watershed — traditional Piscataway territory.

MARK BIGLAND-PRITCHARD is a first-generation Settler of English and Welsh heritage, and a resident in Saskatoon—Treaty 6 territory. A member of Osler Mennonite Church, Mark is an applied physicist and an organizer in the climate justice movement.

ROLAND BOER is a research professor at the University of Newcastle, Australia, and Distinguished Overseas Professor at Renmin University of China, Beijing. The author and editor of over 20 books, Roland's *In the Vale of Tears: on Marxism and Theology* (2014) received the Isaac and Tamara Deutscher Memorial Prize for the most innovative work in the Marxist tradition.

MARCUS BRIGGS-CLOUD is a Maskoke person and son of the Wind Clan. Partnered to Tawna Little, a Kvlice Maskoke person from the Skunk Clan, Marcus enjoys nothing more than conversing in the Maskoke language, especially with his children, Nokos-Afvnoke and Hemokke. A graduate of Harvard Divinity School, Marcus is currently a doctoral candidate in interdisciplinary ecology at the University of Florida and is the director of Ekvn-Yefolecv Maskoke Ecovillage centred in Weogufka, Alabama.

RACHEL AND CHRIS BRNJAS find their home and community in Kitchener-Waterloo, Ontario—the Haldimand Tract of the Haudenosaunee, and traditional territory of the Anishinaabe and Neutral Peoples. Both work in social services, are active members of The Gathering Church, and seek to live out Jesus' radical call of truth, love, justice, and neighbourliness.

SARA BRUBACHER is a Settler Christian living in Kitchener, Ontario—the Haldimand Tract of the Haudenosaunee, and traditional territory of the Anishinaabe and Neutral Peoples. A Clinical Therapeutic Herbalism student in the western tradition with a background in Peace and Conflict Studies and Religious Studies, Sara strives to listen and learn from all animal and plant relations.

WALTER BRUEGGEMANN lives in Cincinnati, Ohio—the traditional lands of the Shawnee—and is the William Marcellus McPheeters professor emeritus of Old Testament at Columbia Theological Seminary. An ordained minister in the United Church of Christ, Walter's numerous books include *The Prophetic Imagination* (1978) and *Money and Possessions* (2016).

CHRIS BUDDEN is a Second Person who lives on the land of the Awabakal people in Newcastle, Australia. A minister of the Uniting Church, Chris works with the Uniting Aboriginal and Islander Christian Congress, has a deep interest in contextual theology and justice for First Peoples, and is lucky enough to be married to Wendy. He is the author of *Following Jesus in Invaded Space: Doing Theology on Aboriginal Land* (2009).

CÉLINE CHUANG is a Settler of colour living on untreatied Coast Salish territories (Vancouver), descended from the migrant Chinese diaspora. She works in the Downtown Eastside, where Indigenous community matriarchs have taught her much about the power of ceremony and womanhood. Her writing has appeared in *Ricepaper*, *Geez*, *The Volcano*, and *The Salt Collective*.

CHRISTINA CONROY is a Settler Christian living in Calgary, Alberta, Treaty 7 territory. Assistant Professor of Christian Theology at Ambrose University, Christina spends her happiest moments being blown around by the wild western prairie winds.

ELLEN F. DAVIS is Amos Ragan Kearns Professor of Bible and Practical Theology at Duke Divinity School, in Durham, North Carolina — traditional territory of the Eno and the Occoneechi peoples. The author of 10 books, Ellen's research interests focus on how biblical interpretation bears on the life of faith communities and their response to urgent public issues, particularly the environmental crisis and interfaith relations.

MIGUEL A. DE LA TORRE is Professor of Social Ethics and Latinx Studies at the Iliff School of Theology in Denver, Colorado — traditional territory of the Arapaho. A former president of the Society of Christian Ethics, Miguel has authored over 100 articles, published 31 books, and wrote the screenplay for the award-winning documentary, *Trails of Hope and Terror*.

JOY DE VITO is a Settler Christian living in the Haldimand Tract, the traditional lands of the Neutral, Anishnaabe, and Haudenosaunee Nations. Co-author of *Lifting Hearts off the Ground: Declaring Indigenous Rights in Poetry*, Joy is learning to listen to the voices of others along with her partner Carlo and their children Micah, Caleigh, and Moriah.

DAVID DRIEDGER is a writer, independent scholar, and Associate Minister at First Mennonite Church in Winnipeg, Manitoba — Treaty 1 territory and the homeland of the Métis Nation. David enjoys living, walking (and running, when his knee allows) in the West End of Winnipeg with his wife, Chantal, and son, Salem.

MUSA W. DUBE is from the Ndebele people, and is an activist-scholar who teaches in the Theology and Religious Studies Department at the University of Botswana. The author and editor of many volumes, including *The HIV/AIDS Bible: Selected Essays* (2008) and *Postcolonial Feminist Interpretation of the Bible* (2000), Musa has worked as an HIV/AIDS and theological consultant for churches and theological institutions in Africa.

RYAN DUECK is a Settler Christian from Lethbridge, Alberta — Treaty 7 territory and the homeland of the Blackfoot Nation — where he serves as pastor of Lethbridge Mennonite Church. Ryan is husband to Naomi and proud father of 16-year-old twins, Claire and Nicholas.

JONATHAN DYCK is a Settler based in Winnipeg, Manitoba — Treaty 1 territory and the homeland of the Métis Nation. He works as the graphic designer for Mennonite Central Committee Canada and has illustrated for a variety of publications including *The Walrus, Maisonneuve*, the *Literary Review of Canada*, and *GUTS Magazine*.

NEIL ELLIOTT is a New Testament scholar, the senior acquisition editor at Lexington/Fortress Academic, and an Episcopal priest in the Diocese of Minnesota. His ancestors included Scottish immigrants who spread the "Restoration" movement as they moved westward from Kentucky to homestead in lands from which the Indigenous nations of the Plains had been driven.

MARC H. ELLIS lives in Cape Canaveral, Florida—traditional land of the Ais and Timucua. A (retired) University Professor of Jewish Studies at Baylor University, Marc is the author and editor of more than 20 books, including *Toward a Jewish Theology of Liberation* (1987), now in its third edition.

DAN EPP-TIESSEN currently teaches Bible at Canadian Mennonite University in Winnipeg, Manitoba, but he hails from Leamington, Ontario, the traditional territory of the Caldwell First Nation. Dan had never heard of the Caldwell until the last few years when the government finally agreed to a land claims settlement. Having recently inherited several arrowheads that his father found on the family farm, Dan is working on repatriating them.

KATERINA FRIESEN is from Mariposa, California—Southern Sierra Miwok land near Yosemite National Park—where she loves hiking with family and friends. Now living on Yokut land in Fresno, California, Katerina works with incarcerated people to plant gardens behind bars through the Insight Garden Program.

LEAH GAZAN is a Lakota woman from Wood Mountain Lakota Nation and is a descendent of a holocaust survivor from Holland. A teacher at the University of Winnipeg, Leah keeps herself busy fighting for social justice across Canada. She is the proud mother of Jakob Henry.

JOSHUA GRACE has Polish and Irish roots and lives in the Delaware River Watershed (Philadelphia)—traditional land of the Lenni Lenape—with his wife Martha and their teenage daughters. While serving as a pastor for Circle of Hope, Joshua recently graduated with an MA in Intercultural Studies from NAIITS, an Indigenous Learning Community.

NORMAN HABEL is a descendant of the Wends who settled in Australia in the 1850s. In the 1990s, Norman worked with Australian Aboriginal elders to create Rainbow Spirit Theology. He is now interested in reading the Bible from ecological, post-colonial, and even Canaanite perspectives. Norman is the editor of *The Earth Bible* series, which seeks to interpret the biblical tradition through an ecojustice lens.

PETER HARESNAPE was born in the United Kingdom and came to Turtle Island with Christian Peacemaker Teams in order to be an ally to Indigenous communities asserting their land rights. He lives with husband, Ken, and housemates, attends Toronto United Mennonite Church, and works as National Coordinator of the Student Christian Movement of Canada.

BOB HAVERLUCK lives on Treaty land where the Assiniboine and Red River meet on their way to the Arctic Ocean. His most recent book, *When God was Flesh and Wild: Stories in Defence of the Earth* (2017), is an imaginative retelling of biblical narratives accompanied by 55 of his tragical comical drawings.

DANIEL HAWK is Professor of Old Testament and Hebrew at Ashland Theological Seminary in Ashland, Ohio — traditional lands of the Wyandot, Erie, Mahican, and Delaware. An ordained minister in the United Methodist Church, Dan is a scholar-activist who writes and speaks on the resonances of the biblical conquest narrative in American national mythology, history, and culture.

STEVE HEINRICHS is a Settler Christian from Winnipeg, Manitoba — Treaty 1 territory and the homeland of the Métis Nation. The director of Indigenous-Settler Relations for Mennonite Church Canada, Steve is a student of activism who loves to march with his partner, Ann, and their children, Izzy, Aiden, and Abby.

JENNIFER HENRY is a Settler who lives under the Dish with One Spoon Wampum Belt Covenant in Toronto. The executive director of KAIROS, Jennifer has worked for 25 years in national and global social justice with Canadian churches and people's movements.

BENJAMIN HERTWIG lives on the untreated territory of the Musqueam, Squamish and Tsleil-Waututh First Nations. He is the recipient of a National Magazine Award, and his debut poetry collection, *Slow War*, was a finalist for the Governor General's Award. He is a PhD Student at the University of British Columbia, working in post-9/11 conflict studies.

WES HOWARD-BROOK lives in the Issaquah Creek watershed out-side Seattle, homeland of the Snoqualmie People. A teacher at Seattle University and the author of *Empire Baptized: How the Church Endorsed What Jesus Rejected* (2016), Wes shares in a ministry of spiritual direction with his wife, Sue Ferguson Johnson (www.abideinme.net).

DERRICK JENSEN is a long-time environmental activist who lives in Crescent City, California, traditional land of the Tolowa. He is the au-thor of more than 20 books, including *Endgame* (2006) and *The Myth of Human Supremacy* (2016). His energies are spent trying to animate resis-tance against industrial civilization, which creates a culture where living beings become objects.

ANITA L. KEITH, Tsi Niká:ien Tekanonniákhwa Nateriíohsera (The One That Dances The War Dance) is of Mohawk/British descent, a mother of three children, and grandmother of four. A former powwow dancer who travelled internationally, Anita is an instructor in the School of Indigenous Education at Red River College, located in Winnipeg, Manitoba—Treaty 1 territory and the homeland of the Métis Nation. She has served in a variety of First Nations ministries and is currently a minister in the Salmon House Diocese, Communion of Evangelical Episcopal Churches.

VIVIAN KETCHUM is from the Wauzhushk Onigum Nation in Treaty 3 territory. A residential school survivor, writer, photographer, and occasional speaker, Viv is an Ikwe woman with a calling to share her Indigenous and Christian beliefs on a road of healing and reconciliation.

SHEILA KLASSEN-WIEBE is a Settler Christian living in Winnipeg, Manitoba—Treaty 1 territory and homeland of the Métis Nation. An Associate Professor of New Testament at Canadian Mennonite University, Sheila enjoys gardening, hiking, canoeing, and making mem-ories with her husband, Vern, and their three young adult daughters.

CARMEN LANSDOWNE is a Heiltsuk woman born in Namgis terri-tory. She is the Executive Director of First United Church Community Ministry Society and First United Church Social Housing Society in Vancouver—located in unceded Musqueam, Squamish, and

Tsleil-Waututh territory. Carmen lives with her partner and their two children in Lummi traditional territory in Ferndale, Washington, and enjoys the quietness of her cross-border commute where she exercises her Indigenous right to see the U.S.-Canadian border as irrelevant.

SUSANNE GUENTHER LOEWEN grew up on Treaty 1 territory in Winnipeg and used Shoal Lake 40 water for decades (including being baptized with it). A Mennonite pastor and theologian, Susanne currently lives with her family on Treaty 6 territory in Saskatoon.

LISA MARTENS is of Dutch Mennonite descent and lives on Treaty 1 territory—the lands of the Anishnaabe, Cree, Métis, Dene and Dakota Nations. Lisa takes care of children and is a graduate student therapist in a master's program for individual, relational, and group therapy at the University of Winnipeg.

SYLVIA MCADAM (Saysewahum) is a *nêhiyaw* (Cree) lawyer, protector, and defender of land and water. A co-founder of Idle No More, Sylvia is a proud mother and grandmother, and the author of *Nationhood Interrupted: Revitalizing nêhiyaw Legal Systems* (2015).

STAN MCKAY is Maskayko (Woodland Cree) from Treaty 5 territory, now living in Treaty 1 territory. A retired minister of the United Church, Stan volunteers with Truth and Reconciliation projects and programs for healing Indigenous families.

CHED MYERS lives in traditional Chumash territory in the Ventura River Watershed of southern California. A member of the Mennonite Church, Ched organizes and educates cross-denominationally around issues of faith and justice with Bartimaeus Cooperative Ministries (www.bcm-net.org). His publications can be found at www.ChedMyers.org.

KYLA NEUFELD is a poet, writer, and editor from Winnipeg, Manitoba—Treaty 1 territory and the homeland of the Métis Nation. She has edited for *Geez* and *Rhubarb Magazine*, and is a frequent contributor to *Prairie Books NOW!* Currently, she is the editor of the *Rupert's Land News*, a monthly publication for the Anglican Diocese of Rupert's Land.

JULIA M. O'BRIEN is a white woman from North Carolina who now lives in Lancaster, Pennsylvania—traditional Susquehannock territory. The Professor of Hebrew Bible/Old Testament at Lancaster Theological Seminary, Julia teaches and writes on the topics of Bible, prophetic literature, gender, violence, and art.

JAMES W. PERKINSON is a Settler Christian at the strait of Detroit—Wawiiatanong for the Ojibwa and Oppenago for the Wendet/Huron. Teaching on colonialism, race, and spirituality at the Ecumenical Theological Seminary, Jim is learning from Indigenous peoples around the globe with his Filipina wife, and acting in the streets against the neo-liberal takeover of the city and its water.

PETER C. PHAN was born in Vietnam and came to the United States as a refugee in 1975. The Ignacio Ellacuria chair of Catholic social thought at Georgetown University, Washington, DC—traditional Algonquin territory—Peter writes extensively on religious pluralism, interreligious dialogue, and migration. His most recent book is *The Joy of Religious Pluralism: A Personal Journey* (2017).

PEKKA PITKÄNEN is Senior Lecturer in the School of Liberal and Performing Arts at the University of Gloucestershire, U.K. He is the author of *Central Sanctuary and Centralization of Worship in Ancient Israel* (2003), *Joshua* (2010), and *A Commentary on Numbers: Narrative, Ritual and Colonialism* (2017). Pekka's research interests include Genesis–Joshua, ritual, anthropological and sociological approaches to the ancient world, migration and colonialism in the ancient Near East, and consideration of how such research relates to contemporary issues.

KWOK PUI-LAN is Distinguished Visiting Professor at Candler School of Theology, Emory University, in Atlanta, Georgia—the traditional home of Cherokee, Apalachicola, Chiaha, and other tribes. She is the author and editor of 20 books, including *Postcolonial Imagination and Feminist Theology* (2005) and *Postcolonial Practice of Ministry: Leadership, Liturgy, and Interfaith Engagement* (2016).

LORI RANSOM is a member of the Algonquins of Pikwàkanagàn First Nation and lives in Toronto on the traditional territory of Huron-Wendat, Mississauga, and Iroquois peoples. Prior to her most recent appointment as Reconciliation and Indigenous Justice Animator with the United Church of Canada, Lori worked on Indigenous issues with the Government of Canada, The Presbyterian Church in Canada, and the Truth and Reconciliation Commission of Canada.

RARIHOKWATS is a member of the Bear Clan and a citizen of the Mohawk Nation at Akwesasne. Since 1965, he has been working for the well-being of Indigenous peoples, advocating for justice around ongoing social, land, and treaty issues.

JOERG RIEGER is a Euro-American theologian who grew up among Methodists and labour unions in Germany. The Distinguished Professor of Theology and Cal Turner Chancellor's Chair of Wesleyan Studies at Vanderbilt University, Joerg studies, writes, and lectures on matters of theology and deep solidarity. Among his books are *Occupy Religion: Theology of the Multitude* (with Kwok Pui-lan, 2012) and *Unified We Are a Force: How Faith and Labor Can Overcome America's Inequalities* (with Rosemarie Henkel-Rieger, 2016).

TAMARA SHANTZ lives with her partner, Gini, their two cats (Isadora and Alex Valentino), along with countless bees, on a small patch of the Haldimand Tract—the traditional lands of the Attawandaron, Anishnaabe, and Haudenosaunee peoples. Tamara is a spiritual director, a pastor with Pastors in Exile (PiE), and teaches on the Enneagram.

TOBIN MILLER SHEARER is a child of God, Cheryl's life partner, and Dylan and Zachary's father. The Director of the African-American Studies Program at the University of Montana and an Associate Professor of History, Tobin lives in Missoula, Montana, on the lands of the Salish Kootenai.

MITZI J. SMITH is an African American Womanist biblical scholar currently living in the Detroit metro area. A Professor of New Testament at

Ashland Theological Seminary, Mitzi's latest publications include *Insights from African American Interpretation* (2017) and *Womanist Sass and Talk Back: Intersectionality, Social (In)Justice and Biblical Interpretation* (2018).

ROBERT O. SMITH is a citizen of the Chickasaw Nation and a pastor in the Evangelical Lutheran Church in America. Originally from Oklahoma, Robert lives in Jerusalem, where he directs academic programs for the University of Notre Dame.

DANIEL L. SMITH-CHRISTOPHER is a Quaker living in Los Angeles, California, where he has been professor of Old Testament at Loyola Marymount University for nearly 30 years, pursuing his keen interest in post-colonial and cross-cultural approaches to Biblical Interpretation. With a profound love for Aotearoa (New Zealand) and a deep respect for Maori culture and people, Daniel and his wife Zsa Zsa are Coordinators of LMU's New Zealand "Study Abroad" program.

KATHY MOORHEAD THIESSEN is a Christian of Irish/English descent living in Winnipeg, Manitoba—Treaty 1 territory and the homeland of the Métis Nation. A member of Christian Peacemaker Teams (Indigenous Peoples Solidarity), Kathy is a student of life and is currently learning Anishinaabemowin in order to have conversations with her Indigenous hosts someday.

SARAH TRAVIS is the Minister of the Chapel at Knox College, and the Director of the Doctor of Ministry Program at the Toronto School of Theology. The author of *Decolonizing Preaching: The Pulpit of Postcolonial Space* (2014), Sarah lives in Oakville, Ontario—the traditional land of the Huron-Wendat, the Seneca, and most recently, the Mississaugas of the Credit River—with her three children, Ben, Ella and Olive.

ROBERT TWO BULLS is an enrolled member of the Oglala Lakọta Oyate and was born and raised on the edge of He Sápa and Makhóšica. An artist, a cleric, a husband and dad, Robert currently works for the Episcopal Church in Mni Sota Makoce, the homeland of his cousins, the Dakota.

REBECCA VOELKEL is a white, lesbian Settler and pastor in the United Church of Christ, who lives in Minneapolis, Minnesota—Dakota and Ojibwe land. As the Director of the Center for Sustainable Justice, Rebecca is a student of religiously-rooted movement-building. With her partner, Maggie, and their 11-year-old daughter, Shannon, Rebecca loves to grow good food and help build the movement around shared tables of communion and struggle.

ALAIN EPP WEAVER is a descendant of German-speaking Mennonite Settlers to Nebraska and South Dakota. The director of Mennonite Central Committee's planning and learning department, and the author of *States of Exile: Palestinian Dispossession and a Political Theology for a Shared Future* (2014), Alain lives in Lancaster, Pennsylvania—traditional territory of the Susquehannock.

GERALD O. WEST is Professor of Old Testament/Hebrew Bible and African Biblical Hermeneutics in the School of Religion, Philosophy, and Classics at the University of KwaZulu-Natal, South Africa. He is also Director of the Ujamaa Centre for Community Development and Research, a project in which socially engaged biblical scholars and ordinary African readers of the Bible from poor, working-class, and marginalized communities collaborate for social transformation. Gerald's most recent publication is *The Stolen Bible: From Tool of Imperialism to African Icon* (2016).

RANDY WOODLEY is an activist scholar and wisdom keeper whose teaching engages an array of concerns from American history to post-colonial theology, community-building to climate change. A legal descendent of the United Keetoowah Band of Cherokee Indians in Oklahoma, Randy and his wife Edith are co-hosts of a permaculture, regenerative teaching farm and community in Newberg, Oregon, housed at Eloheh Village for Indigenous Leadership.

DEANNA ZANTINGH is keeper of the learning centre at the Sandy-Saulteaux Spiritual Centre in Beausejour, Manitoba, Treaty 1. A student of theology and decolonization, some of Deanna's most impactful teachers are friends from Mishkeegogamang First Nation and NAIITS, an Indigenous Learning Community.

A NOTE ON THE TYPE

The body of this book is set in BEMBO, produced by Monotype in 1929 and based on a design cut in 1495 by Francesco Griffo for the Venetian printer Aldus Manutius.

The Scripture verses and headings are set in ALBERTUS, designed by Berthold Wolpe in the 1930s for Monotype. The typeface is named after Albertus Magnus, the 13th-century German philosopher and theologian.